THE ART OF AIKIDO

THE ART OF AIKIDO

Principles and Essential Techniques

BY KISSHOMARU UESHIBA

Preface by Moriteru Ueshiba

Translated by John Stevens

KODANSHA INTERNATIONAL
Tokyo · New York · London

The Founder Morihei Ueshiba

Kisshomaru naturally absorbed many teachings from his father as he was growing up. In the traumatic aftermath of World War II, Kisshomaru believed that the remarkable art of Aikido—established by his father Morihei and based on the best aspects of traditional Japanese culture—could be a positive contribution to the creation of a new society.

Previously, Morihei taught Aikido in archaic, esoteric language, and limited his instruction to a select few. In order to introduce Aikido to the world, Kisshomaru simplified the philosophy and arranged the techniques so that it would be possible for any sincere person to practice Aikido. That effort was a great success—Aikido is now practiced all over Japan and in eighty-five foreign countries. The Aikido ideal of "refining one's mind and body to foster a spirit of harmony" has obviously struck a common chord among the peoples of the world.

It was through the genius of the Ueshiba and the wise administration of the Second Doshu Kisshomaru Ueshiba that today's Aikido came into existence. This book is a compilation of Kisshomaru's writings on Aikido. It will provide the reader with deep insight into both the spiritual and technical dimensions of Aikido. Use this book as an indispensable reference in your daily training, and always keep in mind the words of the Second Doshu Kisshomaru: "Nothing surpasses daily training in Aikido."

Moriteru Ueshiba
AIKIDO DOSHU

AIKIDO PHILOSOPHY

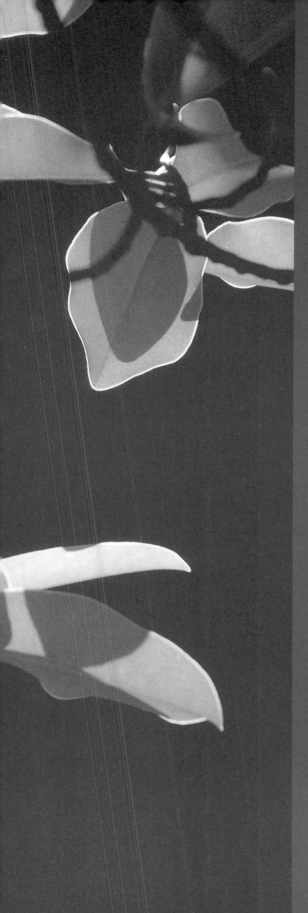

Ki Soku (Energy-Breath)

"Ki is the fullness of life."—Enanji: Huái nán zǐ

Sages of old taught that: "*Ki* is the source of the life force; it is the principle of life that pervades all forms of existence." *Soku*, also known as *iki*, is the core of breath, indispensable for life. Right from the beginning of creation, *ki* and *soku* have been one. From that essential harmony, nature sprang forth in abundance; it is the source of unlimited energy. That essential harmony is the basis of the Way of Martial Valor, and the key to *aiki*, "ideal unity." *Aiki* breath-power is most enhanced when *ki* and *soku* are unified.

Wago (Harmony)

With love fixed in your heart, connect directly to the cosmos

When asked, "What is Aikido?" the Founder Morihei would reply, "The Way to harmonize heaven, earth, and humankind." "Harmony" in Aikido means both to connect oneself to the cosmos (the universal) and to blend with a partner (the particular); in Aikido we draw an opponent into our own sphere of movement in order to guide them. This is true of any of the other arts as well—opposition must always be reconciled to create something of beauty. Here are two *doka* ("Poems of the Way") by the Founder:

> *Aiki*
> Is the base of
> The power of love.
> Let that love
> Ever flourish!
>
> The form of
> This beautiful Heaven and Earth,
> A gift of the Creator.
> We are all members
> Of one family.

Sabaki (Body Movement)

In Aikido techniques, entering and body movement are like the two wheels of a vehicle. Those two elements are manifest in all Aikido techniques. The principle of entering is derived from lethal martial art techniques of the past; the principle of body movement is based on universal patterns, and the unity of *ki*-mind-body. Both principles need to function as one. Expressed in physical form, the body movements of Aikido are circular and spherical. These movements are fundamental to Aikido. An opponent can be drawn into one's sphere by a clean and precise entry; like a spinning top, remain stable at the core, and activate an effective technique. For Aikido techniques, maintaining limitless, circular movements is essential.

THE ESSENCE OF AIKIDO

I. WHAT IS *KI* ?

AIKIDO: a Continuation and Perfection of Japan's Traditional Martial Arts and Ways

From a historical perspective, what is the place of Aikido within the context of the traditional martial arts and ways of Japan? Are there any traditional forms and attitudes from the old-style martial arts and ways that are still preserved in Aikido? To be sure, Aikido is a modern martial way founded by Morihei Ueshiba, but he was influenced by many traditional martial arts and in his new system he incorporated, and breathed new life into, many technical and philosophical aspects of those venerable traditions.

For example, if we consider the technical side of Aikido, we can see many elements—striking, punching, grappling, pressure-point attacks, binding, seizing, Jujutsu arts, throws, weapons, and so on—taken from the old-style martial arts but selected and refined according to Aikido principles. There is also a clear influence of the Tenjin Shinyo Ryu and Kito Ryu Jujutsu systems, and the swordsmanship of the Yagyu Shinkage Ryu; traditions in which the Founder Morihei trained. Thus, it is safe to say that many elements of the traditional Japanese martial arts found new life within the context of Aikido. Furthermore, on a philosophical level, many ancient concepts—yin/yang, hard/soft, physical power/breath-power, body/mind movement, and the like—were adopted into Aikido thought. In this manner, and from any perspective, it can be said that Aikido is a continuation and perfection of the traditional martial arts and ways of old Japan.

The Concept of *Ki*

"Aikido" is comprised of three characters: *ai-ki-do* (合気道). Whether we approach this concept from either a historical or philosophical standpoint, correct understanding of those three words within the ideal Aikido system is essential.

Let us consider the concept of *ki*. Right from the beginning, the notion of *ki* renders one's movements more graceful and free-flowing, echoing the renowned movements of the sword masters of old. The *hakama* has always been an integral element of martial art culture. Unlike Kendo, where the competitors are heavily padded, covered in body armor, in Aikido we maintain the pure, simple fashion of the classical martial artist. This is an external symbol of the spiritual aspirations of Aikido practitioners. As emphasized above, Aikido is primarily an unarmed martial art, employing a one-to-one training method; however, applied techniques are practiced against knife, sword, and staff attacks as well. In such cases, even though some of the techniques are derived from Jujutsu, most of them follow sword movements. When partners are both armed with a sword or staff, we do not refer to those instruments as "weapons." In Aikido, we consider a sword or staff as an extension of the body, moving in harmony with each and every step and turn. In Aikido, a hand-sword is the "sword of no-form;" an actual sword is "an extension of the body." The classical Budo culture of Japan has influenced Aikido in many different ways, and on many different levels, but the primary objective of Aikido is to create a martial way based on harmony and love, and that transcends all other considerations.

III. *KI* AND *TAKEMUSU*

Breath-Power and the Nature of Human *Ki*

The Founder Morihei had two major awakenings that transformed his teaching from a martial art of fighting and contention to a martial Way of human perfection:

(1) Morihei's many intense first-hand experiences on the battlefields of life led to a physical awakening.

(2) Morihei's deep, life-long interest in religion and philosophy led to a spiritual enlightenment.

Awakening (1) will be covered later in the technical section. Here I would like to discuss enlightenment (2), especially the concepts of *kototama*, universal breath-power/individual human *ki*, and *takemusu*.

Kototama

Morihei's interest in the study of *kototama* (also pronounced *kotodama*) was based on his personal research into the nature of breath-power and the generation of *ki* and his varied practical experiences of the breath-power/generation of *ki* continuum. His enlightenment in regard to that continuum led to the creation of Aikido principles and techniques. Since those principles are inherent in Aikido techniques, it is not an absolute requirement for Aikido practitioners to study *kototama* theory, but it is a good idea to have a general idea of *kototama* ideals.

In 1920, Morihei came under the influence of the famous Shinto shaman Deguchi Onisaburo (1871–1948), and he developed a deep interest in ancient Shinto meditation techniques, especially *kototama*, as espoused by Motoori Norinaga (1730–1801), Kiyohara Michihisa, and other mystics. *Kototama* theory is quite complex, but in simple terms it is the "science of sacred sounds." The first appearance of the word *kototama* is in the ancient collection of Japanese verse, the *Man'yoshu*: "Japan is a blessed country where *kototama* is offered." From the earliest times in

Japan, *kototama* was considered the highest and most pleasing form of speech, speech that could only be spoken and understood by people of the highest character and possessed of total integration of body and mind. Furthermore, if mastered, *kototama* was believed to be the secret speech of the gods, a potent source of incantation, magic, and miracle-working. One who truly understood and uttered *kototama* was revered as a person of truth and divinity.

Kototama and the Unification of Man and the Divine

What are "Words spoken by a person of the highest character and possessed of total integration of body and mind?"

First of all, it is not a kind of ordinary, discursive, external manner of speech; it is a profound, pure, intuitive, internal manner of speech. *Kototama* lies beyond the realm of speech, words, voice, sound, or intonation. It is the essence of all those vocalizations. In esoteric science, there are secret sounds such as "Ah" and "Un" (akin to *ki* and *soku* in Aikido) that encapsulate the inner core of sound, the spirit of existence, and the utterances of the gods. Mastery of such sacred sounds enables one to communicate with the unseen powers that drive existence. Unification with the divine promotes the development of *ki/soku* in its purest and most concentrated form, and brings forth the tremendous power of life. This transcendent experience is at the heart of Morihei's teachings on breath-power and the generation of *ki*.

The Miraculous Functioning of *Ki*

Morihei had the remarkable ability to unify himself with the Divine spontaneously, and often went into an Aikido trance. Prior to training, Morihei always sat quietly before the dojo shrine, calming his spirit, setting aright his breath, and concentrating his *ki*. Once his mind was prepared, he was able to perform techniques that seemed miraculous; when he was finished training, Morihei once again sat quietly before the shrine, composed himself, and entered a deep meditative state. He never failed to do this. When he was in meditation, Morihei frequently uttered, in a dramatic manner, such *kototama* as SU, U, or A/UN as an extension of *ki/soku* breath. From these rich personal experiences, Morihei's awareness and had lost their identity. At that junction in history, Morihei believed that Aikido could be a vehicle to lift the heavy burden of defeat from the shoulders of his fellow Japanese, as well as pave the way for a new and peaceful social order. If the fruits of a new discovery only benefit a few select people, it has little social value. A real treasure must be made available to the world at large. This was the beginning of the post-war expansion of Aikido.

The Essense of Budo is Not Fighting

How do people in general view Aikido? One outstanding feature is the large number of female Aikido practitioners. What is the reason for this? Few women care for the big, burly frame developed by many martial artists. Women in general want to remain slim and flexible, and they look for what is bright and self-fulfilling, not what is dark and dangerous.

Many people take up Aikido to promote their physical and mental health. For women, the notion of health includes outer and inner beauty. Aikido for the purpose of self-defense is not much of a factor in attracting new students—perhaps only one in ten. Originally, Budo training was based on these premises: forging one's character, improving one's mind, self-protection, and to maintain law and order in society. When society is in disarray, the primary purpose of Budo is self-protection. If civilization is not established, people need to protect themselves as a matter of course. People do not live in a vacuum, and social conditions greatly affect the way people act. It is no different with the martial arts—sometimes self-preservation is the greatest concern.

Although Budo may have originated in response to battlefield considerations, there are elements in Budo that transcend historical and cultural conditions. Budo was concerned with the critical matter of life and death, a matter crucial for every human being. Certain techniques and teachings that relate to the nature of human existence have universal validity, and are not limited in application to just one time and place. Any true philosophy, east or west, continually inspires each new generation of thinkers.

Considered alongside the long history of the Japanese martial tradition, Aikido is, to be sure, a modern Budo. Yet it is at the same time an ancient Budo. Morihei incorporated the best elements of the traditional martial arts into Aikido, revitalizing them in new forms, and making them more adaptable to modern conditions. Such an approach accounts for Aikido's popularity with female practitioners. The graceful, soft, circular movements of Aikido also appeal to a woman's innate aesthetic sense.

However, it is serious mistake to characterize Aikido as a feminine martial art. The purpose of the martial arts is not to be defeated by an opponent, and Aikido is no exception. The true purpose of Budo is to win without fighting, or contending.

Freedom in Aikido

In regard to human nature, it is much harder to overcome the demons within, than defeat an opponent without. In a society where survival of the fittest is paramount, the martial arts are easy to practice. One trains to defeat an opponent by any means available, and the only criteria for defining a great warrior is one who emerges intact, battle after battle.

Human history, however, shows a preference for civilization. Civilization is the desire for order. Human beings will perish if there is constant warfare, so they long for peace and order. In August 1945, the old order in Japan crumbled. It was time for a new and better order. It was the dawning of the age of Aikido. It was now time to introduce the principles of Aikido to the world at large. In order to understand Aikido, one has to practice. We especially want young people to practice because young people are the future.

The Founder Morihei was an unrivalled master of the 20th century. He adhered faithfully to his principles, and in fact could not act contrary to them, since they were part of his being. Morihei treated everyone the same, as long as a person showed good manners. It did not matter if the person was a high ranking member of society, a business tycoon, or a famous general. Morihei showed no favoritism among his personal students either, even though he had a large number of disciples who were socially prominent or in senior positons in the military. That was Morihei's character. He would demonstrate the techniques to his students personally and show them how to make use of their partner's force. When he taught children, he seemed to become a child himself to make the technique easier to understand. This is the way Aikido should be—direct, unforced, uncalculated. In a word, "free."

Brightness and Flexibility

The Founder Morihei was extremely sensitive. His philosophy was practical yet profound. Morihei's thoughts were not easy to follow; they had to be learned bit by bit. He never tried to explain everything all at once. He did not reject people because of their lack of understanding, nor force people to listen to him. All Morihei asked for was a real interest in Aikido. Such sincere people were welcomed with open arms.

Morihei frequently referred to Aikido as the "Dance of the Gods (*Amakagura*)." This dance, described in the *Kojiki*, was performed by Ame-no-Uzume-no-Mikoto to lure the Sun Goddess out of her cave. It was a dance of liberation, brightness, and bliss. Like this, the goal of Aikido is to dispel all darkness.

I once heard this from the mother of an elementary school student studying Aikido: "Since my son began practicing Aikido he has a much brighter outlook and plays better with his friends." Previously this child had few friends, and was rather sullen and gloomy. Of course, none of his Aikido instructors told him, "Get a better attitude and make more friends." Little by little, the Aikido mind-set influenced the child, and his situation improved. This is how the inner elements of brightness and joy are brought to the surface in Aikido.

The reason one starts to practice is not important. It can be for health or beauty, for fellowship, whatever. Regardless of the reason, the essence of Aikido does not change. In Aikido, we welcome the participation of women. Women who practice Aikido make society stronger and healthier.

Preserving Venerable Traditions in the Midst of Everyday Life

The maturing of a civilization creates certain conflicts, especially in the human heart. People can become consumed by a passion for material gain. Furthermore, goals become obscured, the nature of work changes, people's outlooks shift, and society becomes less stable. All these things increase anxiety. It is important to have goals that don't change, to have a sense of continuity. The fundamental movements of Aikido are circular, round, and flexible, reflecting the endless spinning of the universe. In Aikido, movement and mind are one, so even if the student is not conscious of the principle, it is still naturally absorbed through regular training. The key is constant repetition, learning true Aikido in gradual increments. For those who practice Aikido primarily to improve their health, they will obtain that goal (and many other things) by focusing on the flexible movements of Aikido. In Aikido, even among the highest ranking practitioners, we never see someone who is stiff and overly muscular. The essential quality of Aikido is flexibility. Aikido leads to beauty. Aikido leads to true dialogue. Morihei composed this song of the Way:

> From ancient times,
> Humanities and the martial arts
> Have been the two wheels of the Way.
> Through the virtue of training
> Attain enlightenment of body and mind.

Japan will always be Japan, and there are traditions that will never die. Aikido has its roots in the traditional Budo culture of Japan. However, we should not define Japanese tradition within the narrow confines of nationalism. Aikido is for the entire world, and is now practiced on every continent. Aikido is not something exotic; it is part of the emerging world culture. The genius of Morihei Ueshiba has now become known to the world at large. Pleasantly, powerfully, freely, flexibly—this is how Aikido should be manifested throughout our daily existence.

AIKIDO TECHNIQUE

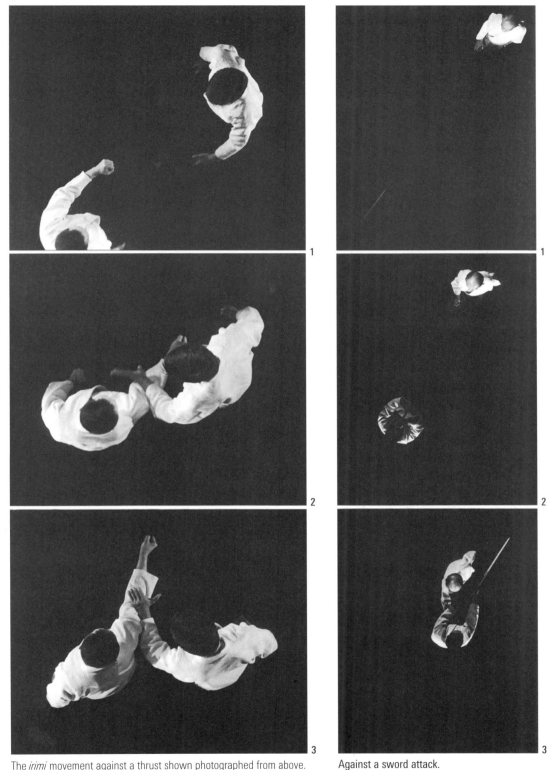

The *irimi* movement against a thrust shown photographed from above.

Against a sword attack.

When a direct blow is delivered, immediately enter to the opponent's dead angle. Photographed from above.

1

2

3

The *irimi* relationship between a sword and *jo*.

Against a *jo* thrust, employ *irimi* to avoid the attack and immediately counterattack with a sword cut.

The relationship between *irimi*, *atemi*, and *jo* movement.

Against a *jo* thrust, enter, apply *atemi*, and throw the opponent.

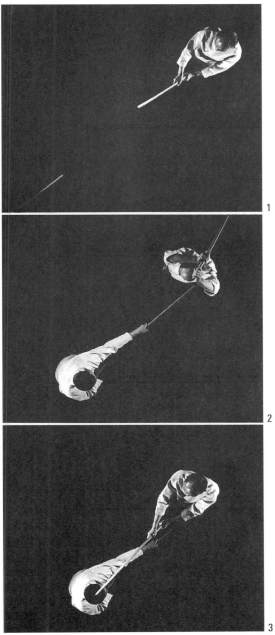

The same technique photographed from above. Note the subtle *irimi* movement to avoid the *jo* attack.

The technique of movement.

Subtly guide your opponent and down him with a *tenchi-nage* throw.

The Relationship between Beauty and Movement

Aikido techniques are based on spherical movement. Harmonization of one's movement with universal movement is the essence of Aikido, and the display of that harmony can be extremely beautiful. *Irimi* coupled with clean, smooth movement lies at the core of Aikido techniques.

The same standing technique shown from a different angle. Note the full extension of the arms and hand-swords.

If properly manifested through the hand-swords, it is possible to effectively employ breath-power against multiple attackers.

When the opponent grabs your wrist, activate breath-power with your hand-sword, break his posture, and down him. Note the skilful use of the *irimi/atemi* principle.

Kokyu-nage (breath-power throw).
The above pictures illustrate how to employ breath-power when your partner attempts a two-handed grab on one arm.

The Relationship between Breath-Power and the Hand-Swords

In Aikido, employment of the hand-swords is primary. Based on the principle that the sword is an extension of the body, when a technique is applied the hand-swords move in unison with the body. In Aikido, breath-power manifested through the hand-swords is very important. Functioning as one, breath-power and hand-swords give life to all the Aikido techniques.

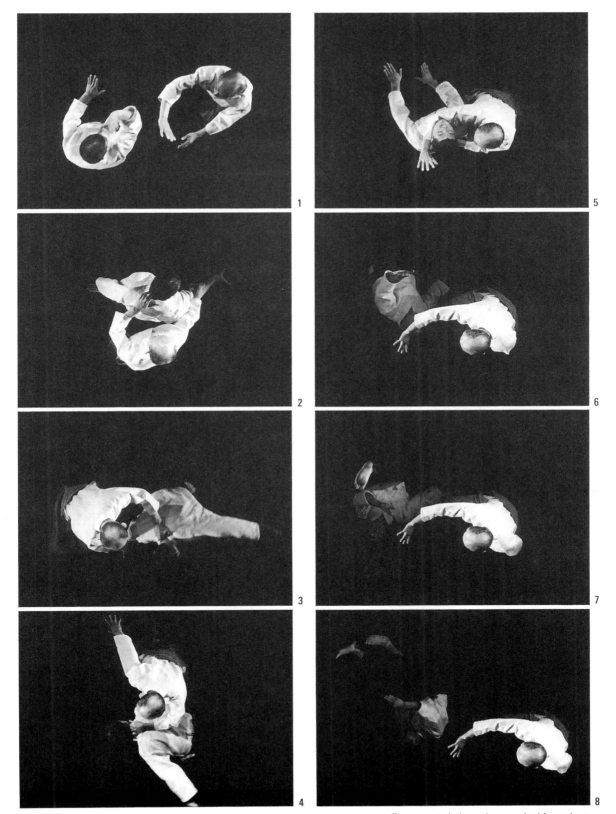

The same technique photographed from above.

Yokomen-uchi irimi-nage.

Employed when your partner attacks with a *yokomen* strike. Keep centered throughout all three turns to break you partner's balance and down him.

Irimi-nage Basic Techniques

Here are three basic *irimi-nage* techniques:

Ushiro ryotekubi-dori irimi-nage.

Your partner approaches from the front and then tries to grab your wrists from behind. Projecting breath-power through the hand-swords, raise both arms, guide your partner around, and employ *irimi-nage* to down him.

Ryote-dori tenkan exercise.

As soon as your partner attempts to grab both wrists, guide him with your hand-swords, take a half-step in, and pivot. Stop the cut half-way, giving your partner's back a good stretch as a preliminary exercise.

The same technique executed with a sword.

When your partner attempts to grab both wrists, guide him around with a sweeping turn and employ the *shiho* sword movement to bring him down.

Katate-dori shiho-nage.

Used when your partner grabs your wrist with one hand. This is the fundamental *shiho-nage* form.

Shiho-nage Fundamental Technique

Hanmi-hantachi katate-dori shiho-nage.

The principles explained on the previous page applied from a seated position.

Against a *yokomen* attack.

Make a big sweeping motion, use your partner's arm as if it was a sword, and apply *shiho-nage*.

Shiho-nage Basic Techniques

Here are some variations of *shiho-nage*. It is essential that such variations be based on experience derived from training. They should not be forced or unnatural.

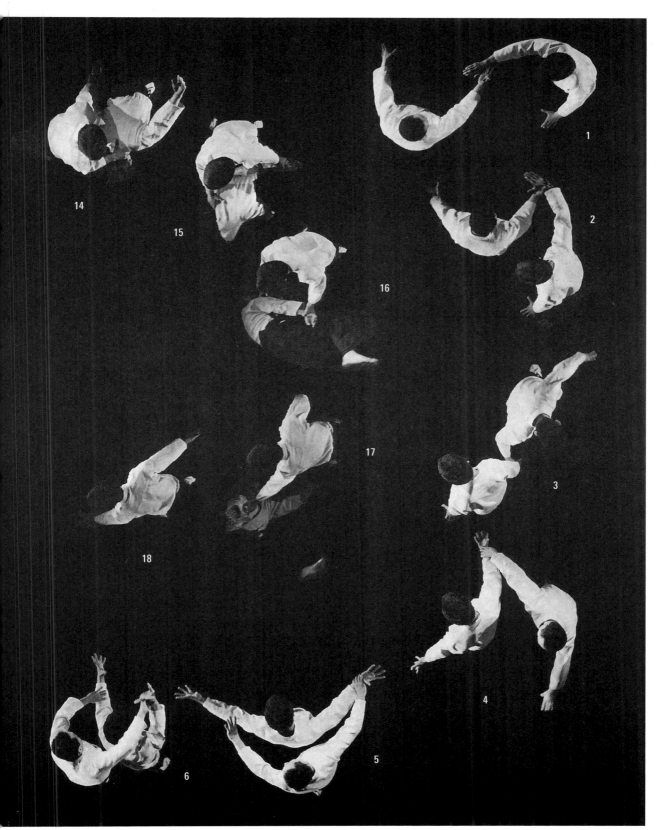

Ushiro ryotekubi-dori kaiten-nage.

When grabbed from behind by both wrists, raise both hand-swords, slide behind your partner, and apply *kaiten-nage* to throw him. The sequence is shown here photographed from above, and there is a montage of the technique at the center.

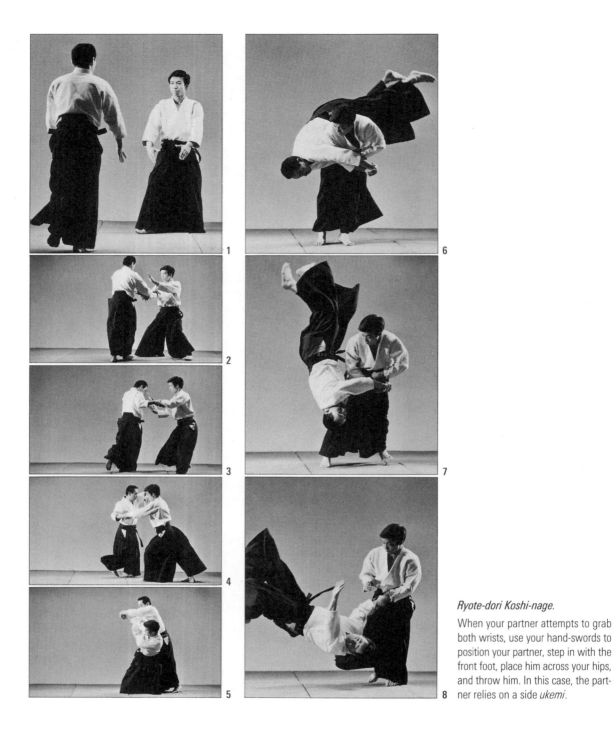

Ryote-dori Koshi-nage.

When your partner attempts to grab both wrists, use your hand-swords to position your partner, step in with the front foot, place him across your hips, and throw him. In this case, the partner relies on a side *ukemi*.

High Throws

In Aikido, we have a number of high throw techniques that employ the hips or arm locks applied from an upper position. It is important that the *ukemi* be timed in unison with the throw. Illustrated here is one form of *koshi-nage* (hip throw) that has many applications.

Dai-ikkyo ude-osae preparatory exercise.

When a *dai-ikkyo* pin is attempted, make a big sweeping turn and lead your partner. The partners alternate performing the exercise on both sides.

BASIC PINNING TECHNIQUES

In addition to throwing techniques, Aikido training emphasizes pinning techniques. Pinning techniques strengthen one's joints, and in general improve the performance of all the other techniques as well.

Pinning Technique Turning Exercise

To be true Aikido techniques, pins need to be executed with flexibility, a smooth flow, and speed.

Dai-nikyo against a knife attack.

When your partner attacks with a knife thrust, immediately enter to his side, apply a *dai-nikyo* lock to his elbow, and disarm him.

Kosa-dori dai-nikyo ura.

when your partner attempts to make a crossover grab of your wrist, immediately control his wrist with the *dai-nikyo* lock applied with a wrapping motion. After bringing him to the ground, make a big turn and apply the *dai-nikyo* pin. Photo 9 shows a close-up of the pin.

Dai-sankyo against a knife attack.

When your partner attacks with a knife thrust, immediately enter and turn while controlling the attacking arm with both your hands. Take hold of his arm with your front hand, step in as shown while applying the *dai-sankyo lock*, bring him down, and take away the knife.

Kokyu-nage employing a big turn prior to throwing to the front with breath-power.

Hanmi-hantachi uchi-kaiten kokyu-nage.

As depicted in the photographs, when your partner attempts to grab your wrist, raise your hand-sword, slide into your partner's side, cut down with your hand-sword, and use his momentum to throw him to the front.

Futari-kake kokyu-nage.

When held on both arms by two attackers, use your hand-swords to make a big circular motion from below, and then extend them out to throw your attackers to the front with breath-power.

The full functioning of true *ki* energy: Mind,
body, and technique as one.

Every April 29th, the date of the Founder Morihei Ueshiba's passing, a memorial ceremony and Aikido demonstration are held at the Aiki Shrine in Iwama. Here Kisshomaru Doshu is shown performing a technique during one such demonstration.

Kisshomaru Doshu practicing *ki* development exercises in the early morning light among the tall cedars on the grounds of the Aiki Shrine.

List of Plates

Acknowledgements

Many people have contributed to various aspects of my researches on the lives of Alice and her husbands during the years I have been working on this project. My thanks are due to William Hamilton-Hinds, of Dame Alice Owen's School, who provided me with notes left by the late Mr Dare, author of the school's history, and, as my principal point of contact with the school, kindly spent a day showing my wife and myself round the buildings; to Vada Hart, and others at the Finsbury Library, for help and advice throughout; to Peter Gwynne-Jones, Garter King of Arms, who has readily answered my questions over many years and provided useful information on heraldic matters; to my cousin, Bruce Hogg, for advice on the same subject; to Ursula Carlyle and Pia Crowley, of the Mercers' Company, for information about the Elkin and Owen connections with the Company; to Guy Holborn, Librarian of Lincoln's Inn, for supplying information about Thomas Owen; to James Lawson, Archivist of Shrewsbury School, on the Owen connection; to James Sewell, City of London Archivist, for advice about City governance; and to Mark Robinson, of the Canadian High Commission in London, for drawing my attention to 18th-century (mis)information on the Robinson pedigree! My brother, Michael Rose, has kindly ferreted out information I needed about Islington Church and my nephew Martin Rose has helpfully commented on the historical background in Chapter 1. My grandson, Tom Preston, sourced the arrow quotations.

I am also indebted to the Machynlleth Tourist Information Centre and to the Clerk of the Egremont Town Council, for historical information; to the Society of Genealogists for giving me access to the late Vera Carpenter's papers; and to the staffs of the Guildhall Library and of the County Record Offices of Northamptonshire, Cumbria and Shropshire for help in dealing with my enquiries.

I am grateful to Charles Dallmeyer, formerly Clerk to the Brewers' Company, for the encouragement he gave me when I first embarked on this project and to his successor, David Ross, for the continuing interest he has shown in it.

Finally, I owe very special thanks to three people who have given me unstinting support and advice throughout the years I have been working on this book: Prue Macgibbon, the Archivist of the Brewers' Company, who has been unfailingly generous in supplying information, answering my queries and commenting on the text as it developed; Joanne Wright, who has cheerfully and patiently decyphered, transcribed and retyped my handwritten drafts and whose comments, particularly on my English and punctuation, have always resulted in improvements, and my wife, Elisabeth, to whom the book is dedicated, whose enthusiasm, appreciation and invariably helpful criticism during a long period of gestation have ensured that the project has eventually been brought to fruition.

While the help and advice offered by all the above is warmly appreciated I should make it clear that I alone am responsible for the conclusions drawn and their presentation.

CLIVE ROSE
June 2005

Preface

Alice looks down on me from her portrait hanging in the dining room of my house in Lavenham. It is the only surviving contemporary portrait of Alice, painted in 1613, the year of her death. It hung in Cransley Hall throughout its occupation by her Robinson descendants and remained there when the Hall was inherited by the grandson of the last Robinson, who was the first Rose of Cransley and my great-great-grandfather. The portrait came into the possession of my father, Alfred Rose, in the late 1920s. He died in 1971 and I inherited it from him on the death of my mother in 1978.

Alice has been willing me to write this book for the past twenty-five years. It was some time before I recognised what she meant and then other commitments prevented me from following her wishes. Only when I was engaged on writing the history of my family, which I completed in 1996, did I come to realise the importance of Alice and her legacy. As her nine-times great-grandson, I had no option but to accept her charge. So in 1999 I embarked on writing the story of her life and those of her three husbands.

This is not quite a story of 'rags to riches', but it is an example of the upward mobility which was fairly typical of 16th-century England. I hope Alice is satisfied with the result. At least she will no longer have any reason to urge me to 'get on with it'. So perhaps she can now rest in peace, or at least let me do so. I fancy the quizzical smile on her face has already assumed a more benevolent aspect.

CLIVE ROSE
Lavenham, 2005

Chronology of the Life and Times of Alice Owen

1523
William ELKIN, Alice's second husband, born Ore, Staffordshire.

1540
Thomas OWEN, Alice's third husband, born Shrewsbury (est).
1544
Henry ROBINSON, Alice's first husband, born Egremont, Cumberland (est).
1547
ALICE WILKES born Islington.
William ELKIN apprenticed Mercer.

1554
William ELKIN admitted to the Freedom of the Mercers' Company.

1533
Princess Elizabeth born.
1534
Act of Supremacy. Breach with Rome.
1536
Queen Anne executed.
1537
Prince Edward born.
1539
English Bible in all Parish Churches.
1540
Thomas Cromwell executed.

1547
Henry VIII died.
Accession of Edward VI
Protestants in power under Protector Somerset.
Chantries suppressed.
1549
Kett's Rebellion.
1552
Cranmer's Second (Protestant) Prayer Book.
1553
Edward VI died.
Accession of Queen Mary I.
Restoration of Roman Catholic liturgy and relations with the Pope.
1554
Queen Mary married Philip of Spain.
Wyatt's rebellion.
1556
Archbishop Cranmer burned at the stake.

1558
The Arrow Incident.
1558
Thomas WILKES, Alice's father, died.

1558
Calais lost to the French.
Queen Mary died.
Accession of Queen Elizabeth I.

1559
Henry ROBINSON apprentice Brewer.
Thomas OWEN graduated as BA at
   Oxford.

1559
Act of Supremacy and Uniformity
   establish Church of England with
   Elizabeth as Supreme Governor.
Revised 1552 Prayer Book.
William Cecil appointed Principal
   Secretary.

1560
William ELKIN's first marriage.

1561
Spire of St Paul's Church destroyed by
   lightning.

1562
Thomas OWEN entered Lincoln's Inn.

1562
Queen Elizabeth survived an attack of
   smallpox.
1563
Statute of Artificers.
1563-1570
John Foxe's *Book of Martyrs*.
1567
Mary Queen of Scots abdicated in
   favour of her infant son, James VI of
   Scotland.

1569
Henry ROBINSON admitted to Freedom
   of the Brewers' Company.
1570
ALICE WILKES married Henry
   ROBINSON.
Lived in Chancery Lane.
Thomas OWEN called to the Bar.

1570
Queen Elizabeth excommunicated by
   Pope Pius V.

1571
Thomas OWEN admitted to Freedom of
   the Mercers' Company.
1572
Thomas OWEN married Sarah
   Baskerville.
Lived in Bassishaw.
1573
Roger OWEN born Bassishaw.
1576
Margaret ROBINSON born Chancery
   Lane.
1577
Ann ROBINSON born.

1577-1580
Francis Drake sailed round the world.

1579
William Elkin, House Warden of the
    Mercers' Company.
1580
Henry Robinson, Warden of the Brewers'
    Company
1581
Alice ROBINSON born.

1582
William ELKIN. Upper Warden of the
    Mercers' Company.
1583
John ROBINSON born.
1584
Thomas OWEN MP for Shrewsbury.
William ELKIN's first wife died.
1585
Henry ROBINSON died.
William ELKIN elected Master of the
    Mercers' Company.
1586
Henry ROBINSON junior born.
ALICE ROBINSON married William
    ELKIN.
Lived in Bassishaw.
William ELKIN elected Alderman and
    Sheriff.
Thomas OWEN bought Condover
    Manor and began building Condover
    Hall.
1587
Ursula ELKIN born Bassishaw.
1588-1592
Thomas OWEN Recorder of Shrewsbury.

1589
Sarah, wife of Thomas OWEN, died.
1590
Margaret ROBINSON eloped with John
    Skinner.
1591
Margaret ROBINSON married John
    Brett.
William ELKIN elected Master of the
    Mercers' Company.
1593
William ELKIN died of the Plague.
Thomas OWEN, Queen's Serjeant.
1594
Thomas OWEN appointed Judge of the
    Court of Common Pleas.

1581
Edmund Campion, Jesuit martyr, hung,
    drawn and quartered.

1584
Virginia established by Walter Raleigh.

1587
Mary Queen of Scots executed.
1588
Defeat of Spanish Armada.
Robert Dudley, Earl of Leicester, died.

1590
Spenser's *Faerie Queene*.

1595
ALICE ELKIN bought Cransley estate
    and manors from Thomas Cecil.
ALICE ELKIN married Thomas OWEN.
1596
Thomas OWEN elected Master of the
    Mercers' Company for 1597.
1597
Roger OWEN MP for Shrewsbury.
John ROBINSON, Alice's son, died.
1598
Thomas OWEN died in Bassishaw,
    buried in Westminster Abbey.
Alice ROBINSON married John
    Washbourne.
1599
Ann ROBINSON married Robert Rich.
1601
Roger OWEN MP for Shropshire.
Also in 1605/10/14.

1604
Roger OWEN of Condover knighted.

1609
ALICE OWEN's almshouses established
    in Islington.
Ursula ELKIN married Sir Roger
    OWEN.
Lived at Condover.
1611
Henry ROBINSON married Mary
    Glover.
Lived at Cransley.
1613
ALICE OWEN's School opened in
    Islington.
ALICE OWEN died in Bassishaw and
    buried in St Mary's Islington.
Brewers' Company made Trustees of her
    Foundation.
1614
Henry ROBINSON of Cransley
    knighted.
1617
Sir Roger OWEN died at Condover.

1595
Shakespeare's *A Midsummer Night's
    Dream* and *Romeo and Juliet*.

1598
William Cecil (Lord Burghley) died.
Philip II of Spain died.

1601
Last Elizabethan Poor Law.
Earl of Essex executed for treason.
1603
Death of Queen Elizabeth I.
Accession of James VI of Scotland to
    English throne as James I.

1605
The Gunpower Plot.

1611
King James' Bible (Authorised Version)
    published.

Chapter 1

The England of Alice's Childhood

Alice was born in 1547, the year in which Henry VIII died. Her eventful life spanned the tumultuous reigns of Henry's three children. Despite her humble origins and the unremitting religious and political upheaval of the period, Alice was to rise to great wealth and position which would enable her to end her life on a high level of achievement in the relatively calmer waters of the reign of the first Stuart King.

This Chapter describes Henry's legacy and the England Alice knew in her childhood during the reigns of two of his children, Edward and Mary. Many good things as well as the much-publicised bad ones occurred in Henry VIII's reign. He presided over a religious and administrative revolution which had far-reaching effects on life in England not only throughout Alice's lifetime but well beyond, down to the present day. Yet the King who started his reign 38 years earlier with so much promise as a scholar, poet, musician and sportsman ended it as a cruel and bloated autocrat whose courtiers were too fearful to tell him he was dying. His self-indulgence, financial recklessness and determination to cut a figure on the world stage nearly brought his country to ruin.

Edward VI and Mary Tudor brought even more turmoil to the English people. The former's reign was a period of incompetence and bigotry under a boy King guided by two self-seeking 'Protectors', and the latter's one of disaster under a middle-aged Queen whose reputation was forever tarnished as a result of her religious fanaticism and her misguided infatuation for her Spanish husband.

Alice's adult life was spent in the long reign of Henry's second daughter, Elizabeth, which was less hazardous for those who took care to avoid the pitfalls. The age of Gloriana was infinitely more inspiring than that of either of her siblings.

England in the mid-16th century was predominantly rural. Out of a population of about three million – a quarter of the size of France – no more than one fifth lived in towns. Of these London was far and away the largest and the richest, with a population of about seventy thousand in the City itself and a further thirty thousand or so in Westminster, the centre of the Court and Government, and the suburbs north of the Thames. Next in size came York, capital of the north, Norwich, a great centre of the cloth trade, and the major seaport of Bristol, all with around twenty thousand. Below these no other town exceeded five thousand. The population was thinly spread and most of the roads were not much better than what would today be described as cart tracks, which is literally what they were. Horse or oxen drawn carts were used for carrying goods, other than commodities which could be transported by sea, such as coal from Newcastle to London, known from its method of transport as 'sea coal'. Horses were the only form of 'people-carrier'; it was not until much later in the century that carriages were introduced and then only affordable by the rich. The danger of being robbed on the road was such that no gentleman or indeed yeoman would venture on a journey without being armed with sword and dagger. Even on the few miles across open country between Islington, the village of Alice's birth and childhood, and the City of London, where she spent most of her life, no man would risk travelling alone unarmed.

The majority of the population earned their living from the land and even people whose main employment was urban or semi-urban often farmed smallholdings as tenants. Alice's father was one of these, and the fathers of her first two husbands were both tenant farmers. Most of the industry outside London was agriculture-related, as for example weaving, the curing of hides and the production of implements required for farming.

The agricultural products included fruit, such as apples and cherries, grown in Kent, grain – wheat, barley and rye – for which the principal source was the arable land of the Midlands and East Anglia. Hops were starting in Kent and hemp, for canvas and rope, was also grown in the eastern counties. Cattle were widespread, especially in the hill country in the west of England. Meat and hides were exported, but by far the largest agricultural product and the basis of the country's export trade in the first half of the 16th century was wool. It was woven into white cloth and exported unprocessed to the continental markets, of which the principal one was Antwerp. Sheepmeat was also exported, but the cloth trade was so profitable that much arable land was converted to pasture in many parts of the country, especially in the east Midlands and East Anglia, to accommodate the vast expansion of the sheep population for the main purpose of producing wool.

Those who were in a position to do so took every possible means to profit from this booming trade. Besides the natural motive of increasing their wealth, they were faced with the new phenomenon of inflation. In the first half of the 16th century the cost of living more than doubled and the price of food nearly trebled. This was an experience which had been virtually unknown in the previous century when men were used to thinking in terms of a just price, fixed by some immutable law, for everything. These two factors, the booming trade in wool and the unprecedented rise in prices (the reasons for which are considered below), had effects which varied according to the status of the individual countryman. Landlords did all they could to increase the return from their land. Besides turning over arable land to pasture, they frequently enclosed for their own use the common land and waste-land beyond the cultivated area on the outskirts of villages which were farmed by the villagers. This deprived the common people of the rights of grazing for their livestock. Then they raised the rents of their tenants where this was possible. Yeoman freeholders were secure in their tenure; so were most copyholders on long leases with fixed rents. But short leaseholders and tenants-at-will were hard hit and many who were unable to pay were evicted from their leased property. Sometimes the landlords simply took over strips of the villagers' cultivated land for their own use. The expansion of sheep farming made no contribution to increasing employment, so the actions of the landlords, often taken for no more reason than to defend their own standard of living, had the effect of depriving the landless labourers and insecure tenants of their means of livelihood. Some of the former joined the large body of vagrants who presented a constant danger to travellers on lonely country roads. Others including many of the smaller tenants – lesser yeomen and husbandmen, – who could not make a living out of their smallholdings or find employment on the estates of the squires or the farms of well-to-do yeomen, migrated to the towns, especially London, in search of work or simply to beg.

The grievances of the rural poor brought about a simmering discontent through the country during, and beyond, the first half of the 16th century. Such outbursts as Robert Kett's rebellion in Norfolk in King Edward's reign were repeated on a smaller scale in many places. They were not supported by the landlords, whose interests were threatened by them, and, in the absence of any co-ordinated movement, were repressed, often ruthlessly. They were symptomatic of a situation which had the general effect of making the rich richer and the poor poorer.

One feature of the period was the enhanced status of the rural gentry, to whom might be added the newly ennobled or gentrified professional classes who from humble origins had by their own abilities risen to high office and wealth under the Tudors, at the expense of the great nobles whose feudal dominance of rural England had been largely eroded by the loss of their estates after the Wars of the Roses. Many of the latter sought to retain influence or at least status by spending their time in proximity to the Court and Government where they hoped to secure favours. The 16th century also saw the rise of the yeomen who, by hard work and thrift which was their characteristic, became virtually equivalent in status, and often superior in wealth, to the squires. Manor houses of Tudor origin in all parts of the country bear witness to the rise in wealth and status of these new rich. It was from all these classes that the Justices of the Peace were appointed, who exercised judicial and administrative power on behalf of the Crown. From the early part of the 16th century onwards the J.P.s became the backbone of local government in the Shires. Thomas Owen, Alice's third husband, was to hold this appointment in several counties in the latter part of the century.

The effects of inflation were felt not only by the rural poor but also by many urban dwellers. With the exception of those fortunate enough to own farms or estates outside London, the ordinary urban worker had no means of augmenting his income to compensate for the rise in prices, and he was therefore subjected to the full force of inflation. How had this happened? The underlying causes have been ascribed to the steep increase in population, especially the urban population, at a time when food production and opportunities for employment remained virtually static and at the same time the demand for land (and therefore its price) had grown strongly. The problem was exacerbated by Henry's profligate expenditure and Wolsey's inept financial management.

Henry VIII had inherited from his prudent but parsimonious father a full treasury and a stable economy. This inheritance had been dissipated by Henry's extravagant lifestyle and overseas ventures. He embarked on a series of costly and unnecessary wars, of which the final one against France ended only a few months before his death. To pay for this Henry contracted vast foreign loans at a high rate of interest which saddled his successors with a crippling burden of debt. At the same time he ordered a disastrous second debasement of the silver coinage which led to soaring price rises. The poor, as always, were the main sufferers from a situation which lasted for most of the century, at least until they enjoyed some relief from the great Elizabethan Poor Law. The Crown and Government benefited from the revenues accruing from the dissolution of the monasteries and sale of their estates to the already wealthy rural squires and other country landowners. This was not enough to meet the level of expenditure required to maintain the standard expected of (and by) the Crown. So recourse was had by Elizabeth to the one class whose wealth remained unaltered, and indeed enhanced, by the economic storm. This was the great City Companies, such as the Mercers, in which Alice's second husband, William Elkin, was a leading light, the Brewers, the trade in which her first husband, Henry Robinson, made his fortune, and others who were often called upon for grants or 'loans'.

Henry took little interest in the minutiae of government. He was fortunate in being served, for the greater part of his reign, by two able administrators who were the principal architects of the revolutionary changes he bequeathed to his successors. Each of them wielded too much power to be popular with their peers and their power ultimately depended on the King's favour, on losing which each in turn lost his office and his life. But their legacies were important to the lives of the ordinary people of England and therefore deserve brief reference here.

The first of the two, Cardinal Thomas Wolsey, introduced, or at least developed, major improvements in the administration of justice. Though without any formal legal training, he ensured that the Courts over which as Lord Chancellor he presided dealt promptly with cases before them and that their judgements were enforced. He established a new Court of Requests expressly to deal with complaints from the common people of the country. He thus gained friends among the humble and uninfluential people whose rights were often upheld and enforced, and was disliked by the rich and powerful who thought themselves above the law and reacted unfavourably when forced to comply with judgements which went against their interests.

Such people were in any case only too ready to find cause for grievance against the overwheening Chancellor and Cardinal. Alhough he was resented by the professional lawyers who felt themselves sidelined by this powerful amateur, his legacy of impartial justice endured and, by the time Thomas Owen was elevated to the Bench as a Judge of the Court of Common Pleas, the rivalry between the Chancellor's Courts and the traditional Common Law Courts had been largely resolved.

Thomas Cromwell, who ranks as one of the greatest administrators of the 16th century, made major contributions in two areas which affected Alice and her family. The first was his reform of the structure of Government. The members of the smaller and more efficient Privy Council which he created sat in Parliament as, in effect, the Government Front Bench and the principle was established that national sovereignty rested not on the King alone but on a partnership between the Crown and Parliament. The latter could criticise and in theory reject proposals made by the Crown. Although under Henry it was unlikely that the Crown would not in the end prevail, the way was open for such noted rebels as Alice's son-in-law, Roger Owen, a well-known Radical, at the beginning of the next century publicly to oppose the King's policies with relative impunity. It is not too much to see in this reform the seed of the eventual evolution, after many reverses, of the modern system of Cabinet Government and Constitutional Monarchy.

All these events affected Alice and her family in one way or another, and Wolsey's and Cromwell's reforms had both short and long-term consequences for the government of the country. But it was the religious conflict that had most effect on the lives of the English people of all levels of society throughout the 16th century.

The religious revolution in England was not a response to demands made by ordinary people, most of whom were firmly attached to the Catholic faith and liturgy. It was the result of decisions taken by reformist councillors, bishops and academics whose views prevailed over the traditionalists because they suited the special interests and vanity of the King. Its components were complex and diverse. The influence of Protestant doctrines inspired by Martin Luther and others, resentment of the Pope's involvement in judicial and administrative matters in England, jealousy of the wealth of the higher dignitaries of the Church, the dual allegiance of bishops and clergy to Pope and King and the financial exactions demanded by Rome all combined to set the scene for a showdown. The spark that lit the tinder was ultimately the King's realisation that the only way he could obtain the annulment of his marriage to Queen Catherine was to expel the power of the papacy from England. The breach with Rome took place in the 1530s. Was the Church of England to which the English Reformation gave birth Catholic or Protestant? A further quarter of a century was to elapse before it was possible to attempt an answer to this question.

During the early years of the 16th century the Wilkes family in Islington, the Robinsons of Cumberland, the Elkins of Staffordshire and the Owens in

Shrewsbury, and their contemporaries throughout the country, went to Mass every Sunday and often on Holy Days as the Catholic Church bid them do. They did not necessarily receive the Eucharist every week and when they did they partook only of the consecrated bread which they were taught was invested with the physical properties of the Body of Christ. The priest, who consecrated the elements but alone drank the wine, recited the service in Latin which the greater part of the congregation (and often the priest himself) did not understand. He faced the altar at the east end of the church and had his back to the people so that he was barely audible to his congregation. The latter had no access to the scriptures which were also in Latin and for their knowledge of the Christian faith were wholly dependent on what the priest chose to tell them. They believed, and most of them were probably genuine in their belief, that this regular act of devotion benefited their immortal souls and they expected to gain credit hereafter by the adornment of their churches with images, sacred relics and lavish ornaments. The priest's God-given authority to celebrate the Mass and administer the other sacraments of the Church gave him a power over their lives to which they submitted, however reluctantly.

While this authority was not questioned, many priests forfeited the respect of their parishioners because of their perceived corruption, immorality, greed and often their ignorance. They were in fact seen as embodying the vices people recognised in themselves but did not expect to find in their priests. This is of course a sweeping generalisation; there were many devout and honest parish clergy. But, perception or reality, it produced a combination of secular anti-clericalism and religious orthodoxy. Added to this was resentment of the powers of the church courts whose jurisdiction in matrimonial and testamentary cases had gradually been extended to cover many other aspects of people's lives, and whose judgements were often arbitrary and accompanied by exorbitant fines, from which the only appeal was to Rome.

The majority of members of Parliament, whether Reformists or not, shared or were persuaded to share the objections of the King and his Councillors to the powers exercised by the Pope in England. So the legislation passed at the request of the King, acting on Cromwell's advice, to give effect to a complete break with Rome and to make Henry Supreme Head of the Church as well as of the State was generally welcomed by the laity. The requirement which soon followed, that a copy of the Bible in English (the Matthew Bible, based on the previously banned translation by Tyndale and Coverdale) should be made available to the public in all parish churches, was seen as a major step in the liberation of the people from rule by the clergy. The next cautious step towards Protestantism, the destruction of images and relics, to which people had a strong emotional attachment, was less well received. But Henry, who remained at heart attached to the orthodox faith, became alarmed at the spread of heresy and made it a capital offence to question the principal elements of Catholic doctrine, including the 'Real Presence' in the Mass and priestly celibacy. After Cromwell's fall he was persuaded by his conservative Councillors of the potentially subversive effect of unrestricted access to and free discussion of the Scriptures, and directed that the English Bible should be read only by the clergy, nobles and gentry – and denied to all below 'gentle rank', including women, children and apprentices! Roman Catholics who refused to acknowlege the Royal Supremacy were executed and Protestants who denied the doctrine of transubstantiation were burned at the stake. The King's vacillations must have been confusing even to those ordinary churchgoers who understood what was happening. At the time of Henry's death the faith into which Alice was baptised could best be described as Catholicism without the Pope.

This was where most people were content to see it remain, certainly in the north and in the south-west of the country, where even the changes made so far had caused considerable discontent. They were totally unprepared for the wave of Protestant iconoclasm introduced by Protector Somerset, with the cautious support of the Archbishop of Canterbury, Thomas Cranmer, which grew in intensity as the young King's reign went on. Crucifixes were smashed, paintings and statues of the Virgin Mary were removed from churches, the sacred vessels used in the Mass were banned, altars were replaced by plain wooden tables on which only two candles were permitted and the endowed Chantries in which prayers were said for the souls of the donors and their families were abolished and the revenues appropriated to the Crown. These measures were enforced rigorously in London and the south-east and more half-heartedly elsewhere. They were hated not only by many of the clergy, who were in the main conservative, but also by the laity all round the country, especially in rural parishes. Catholic loyalties were strong among many north country families, such as the Robinsons in Yorkshire and Cumberland, the home of Alice's first husband. In Shrewsbury, the parishioners of St Chad's, the parish church of the Owen family, had little enthusiasm for reform.

The redeeming feature of Edward's reign was the reformed liturgy intro-duced by Cranmer. His first English Prayer Book, which contained only two daily services, Matins and Evensong, in place of the eight of the Catholic rite, and many new English prayers in the Mass, now also called Holy Communion, was too much of a compromise to satisfy either Catholics or Protestants. Some Catholic priests chose to resign rather than to use it. One was James Robinson, the Vicar of St Mary's, Islington, the parish church of the Wilkes family in which Alice had been baptised. The second version, in 1552, omitted all concessions to the Catholics and, though not fully meeting their demands, was sufficiently reformist to be acceptable to the Protestants. The laity were to receive the sacrament in both kinds at Holy Communion (no mention now of the Mass) and, in place of the Catholic doctrine of transubstantiation, Cranmer enunciated the distinctively Anglican doctrine of Christ's spiritual presence in the consecrated bread and wine, a crucial distinction for the sophisticated but probably incomprehensible to most ordinary communicants. The Prayer Book was prescribed by Parliament under the Act of Uniformity for use in all parish churches and anyone absenting himself from the Sunday services was liable to imprisonment. Cranmer's next step was the promulgation of 42 Articles of Faith, which owed much to Protestant influence and which might fairly be described as the constitution of the Church of England. This gave some comfort to the many confused churchgoers who already found it difficult to exercise the unaccustomed freedom of conscience which was incumbent on them now that they had direct access to the scriptures.

This was the high water mark of Cranmer's reforms. Though they were not yet fully implanted in the hearts of an essentially conservative populace, English people were becoming resigned to the fact that, like it or not, they would have to learn to live with them. Within months of the adoption of these reforms the young King Edward died and, after the Duke of Northumberland's abortive attempt to install his daughter-in-law Lady Jane Grey on the throne, King Henry's elder daughter, the devoutly Catholic Mary, was proclaimed Queen. Her advent was widely welcomed as presaging a return to the old familiar religion, and so it did. The laws enacting Cranmer's reforms were repealed and the Latin Mass restored. The crucifixes, images of the Virgin Mary and saints and vessels which in many parishes had been hidden by the faithful during the Protestant interdiction were replaced. The revival of the rule of celibacy meant that many clergy had to choose between their livings and their wives. The breach with Rome was healed and absolution was granted by the Pope. All this was done with the sincere though obsessive purpose on the part of the Queen to save the souls of her subjects from heresy. It led her agents to apply penalties for any deviation from Catholic orthodoxy with extreme cruelty, with the result that much of the initial goodwill towards Mary was soon dissipated. Her principal instrument in London, Bishop Bonner, personally supervised the torture by the rack of many who were suspected of heresy or treason. Those convicted were burned at the stake, a total of three hundred in all; many more suffered excruciating pain and even mutilation. Among those martyred were Archbishop Cranmer, and Bishops Latimer and Ridley, but most of them were humble folk as many of the leading Protestants had fled the country.

Mary compounded her unpopularity by her marriage to Philip of Spain and the consequent subordination of English to Spanish interests. The final blow to the diminishing loyalty of her subjects was the loss of Calais, a disaster more symbolic than practical, which resulted from England being drawn, as an ally of Spain, into yet another unnecessary war against France. On her death in 1558 Mary was little mourned.

Elizabeth's accession was greeted with relief and enthusiasm. Her immediate priority, with William Cecil's sage advice, was to achieve a religious settlement. This was reached in the following year with support from the House of Commons but against considerable opposition from the Lords where the Marian bishops were powerful. The new Act of Uniformity reinstated Cranmer's 1552 Prayer Book with some modifications, and the Monarch's title was revised from 'Supreme Head' to 'Supreme Governor' of the Church, a change which implied secular rather than ecclesiastical control. A few years later the Articles of Faith (reduced to 39) were re-enacted by Parliament. This was by no means the end of religious controversy in Elizabeth's reign (and Alice's lifetime) and thereafter. However, most English people accommodated themselves, with a sigh of relief, to the Church of England by law established, without giving much thought to the question whether it was Catholic or Protestant. The liturgy and doctrine then enacted have survived with remarkably few changes to the present day.

Chapter 2

Islington and the Wilkes Family

Alice was one of three children of Thomas Wilkes by his first wife. The eldest child was Margery and Robert was probably the second. Thomas was an 'Innholder' in Islington, where he lived all his life. He married a second wife, Margaret, by whom he also had three children. He died and was buried at St Mary's Church, Islington, in February 1558. This much is known from Thomas's Will.[1] Records of baptisms, marriages and burials at St Mary's for this period are non-existent. So factual evidence about the early years of Thomas Wilkes's family is sparse. But by making some reasonable assumptions from future recorded events, it is possible to construct a credible picture.

Alice was almost certainly the youngest of the children of Thomas's first marriage; the qualification is necessary because of the complete absence of any records of their dates of birth. That Alice was born in 1547 can be deduced from her known age of 66 at the time of her death on 27 October 1613.[2] Her elder sister, Margery, was married in 1559. Assuming she was then 19, a normal age for a girl to marry, she would have been born in 1540. Robert's marriage, at a later age, is no guide. But he was evidently a teenager by the time of his father's death, which would place his date of birth sometime between his two sisters. Their mother probably died soon after Alice was born and the children by Thomas's second marriage were all well under ten by the time of his death. Their names were not mentioned in his Will, but only two other Wilkes's have been identified in the Islington parish records up to the end of the 16th century. One is John Wilkes, referred to as a 'kinsman' in Robert's Will; the other is Christopher, a vintner (licensee of a wine-tavern), who was buried in 1603 and whose only surviving child was Margaret (perhaps named after his mother). So it is possible that these were two of the children of Thomas's second wife, Margaret, and thus Alice's half-brothers. But apart from the fact that they spent their childhood years in the same household as Alice, they are not known to have played any further part in her life.

Alice's story begins and ends in Islington. Her affection for the place of her birth was strong and she maintained her connections with it throughout the whole of her life. Islington, often known in the early part of the 16th century by its ancient name of Iseldon, was a country village about two miles north of the City of London. It was situated on high ground and separated from the metropolis by fields and open countryside. The village has been described as 'a salubrious pleasure resort'; it certainly provided a welcome relief from the crowded, noisy and dirty streets of the City of London and was also a favourite haunt of the nobility and gentry from the City of Westminster. Several noble families and rich merchants had country houses in Islington parish which, besides the main settlement, included Canonbury, Holloway, Highbury, Tollington, Newington Green and Stroud Green, a total area of a little over 3,000 acres bounded to the north by Hornsey and to the south by Clerkenwell.

Henry VIII was a frequent visitor; he held a monopoly for the hunting of hares, partridges, pheasants and herons in all the country between Westminster and Hornsey, which included the whole parish of Islington. 'King Henry's Walk' remains today as a reminder of his fondness for these excursions. In nearby Newington Green, Henry Percy, by then Earl of Northumberland and securely, if not happily, married, had a house, from which he is said to have written to the King in 1536 denying, almost certainly falsely, that any 'precontract' had existed between himself and Anne Boleyn in the 1520s; he compounded the offence by confirming the denial in a sacred oath (sworn under pressure) before the two Archbishops.[3] Lord Berners, Lieutenant of Calais, owned Barnesbury Manor until his death in 1533, when it passed shortly afterwards to Robert Fowler, Vice-Treasurer of Calais and to his descendants. In Islington, as elsewhere, politics and religion often determined the ownership of property. The Manor of Canonbury is a not untypical example. Situated just to the north of the main settlement, it was originally owned by the Priors of St Bartholomew but passed to the Crown on the dissolution of the monasteries. Henry VIII granted it to Thomas Cromwell, as Earl of Essex, who however lost both the manor and his head in 1540. Edward VI gave it to John Dudley, Earl of Warwick, but it returned to the Crown on his execution in 1553 and Queen Mary granted it to the Catholic Lord Wentworth. His family's ownership did not long survive the accession of Queen Elizabeth by whom it was passed to the Spencer family.

Elizabeth used to ride out to Islington to visit Sir John Spencer, Sir Thomas Egerton, Sir Francis Bacon, the Fowler family and others. The Earls of Leicester and Essex (Robert Devereux) also had houses there at some time. Sir Walter Raleigh, who held the authority for licensing taverns throughout England, was an habitué of the Islington inns, especially the *Old Pied Cow* on the Green. The story is told of him that, when sitting smoking a pipe of the tobacco he had recently introduced into England, a habit still unfamiliar to Islington, he called for a tankard of small ale; the servant seeing the smoke rising from Raleigh's pipe, threw the ale in his face and shouted 'Fire! Help! Sir Walter has studied till his head is on fire and the smoke burst out of his mouth and nose.'[4] In short, the impression given is that anyone who was, or aspired to be, anyone in 16th century England made it his business, and his pleasure, to establish some connection with this fashionable village. Indeed to such an extent did the country houses of these rich Londoners encroach on the agricultural and recreational land of the parish that towards the end of the century an attempt was made to ban any further building within three miles of London, but evidently with little effect.[5]

Islington was much more than a pleasant resort for the rich and powerful 'weekenders', holiday-homers and day visitors. The main settled area was situated round the High Street and Islington Green, from the junction of St John's Road and Goswell Road in the south and northwards along Upper Street as far as Hopping Lane (which in those days ran from Upper Street to Newington Green) and along Lower Street (now Essex Road) as far as Cross Street. It is difficult to arrive at an accurate figure for the population of the parish. The only available information comes from the records of 'houselings' (Easter communicants) at St Mary's Church in 1548. Unfortunately the sources do not agree. One account gives 240; another quotes the number as 440.[6] These figures suggest a total population of between 500 and 900; it is possible that the lower figure could apply to the settled area between the Green and the Church in Upper Street and that the higher figure might include all those living in the outlying hamlets and farms which took up much of the land to the north-east and north-west of the settled area. At any rate outside this area Islington was sparseley populated. At the beginning of the 19th century meadows and pasture accounted for about 2,700 acres of the total parish, with only the remaining 330 acres devoted to houses, gardens and businesses: this proportion had probably changed little since the 16th century.

Agriculture was the principal occupation and a major source of income in Islington. The parish was famous for its production of the full range of dairy products – milk, cream, butter and cheese; these, with hay from the pastures on which the cattle grazed, supplied the ever expanding needs of the London market. The rapidly increasing population of the City also created a growing demand for corn. To meet this farmers were forbidden by law to convert to grass land which had previously been arable, and several who disregarded it were taken to court.[7] Despite the pressure to turn to corn-growing however, most of the large farms and the smallholdings of Thomas Wilkes and others like him continued to be based on pasture for livestock. So Islington maintained its reputation for the quality of its dairy products. These won high praise from the gentlemen accompanying Queen Elizabeth on her progress to Kenilworth in 1575, when she passed through Islington. In an entertaining discussion about suitable arms for the parish, the last word went to the gentleman who proposed:

> Three milk tankards proper, in a fielde of cloouted cream, three green cheeses upon a shealf of cake-bread. The fyrmenty boll and horn spoonz, cauz their profit comes all by horned beauty, supported by a mare with gold bak and therefore still covered with a panniell, frisking her tall for flyes and her filly fole naying after her dam for suk.

And for motto: 'Lac, caseus infans; that is, fresh cheese and cream, and the common cry that their milk-wives make in London streets betwixt Easter and Whitsuntide.'[8] It was a good try, but no-one proposed that it should be adopted!

Islington's other main occupation was innkeeping, which was Thomas Wilkes's profession. The village was noted for its many inns, which served the needs both of visitors from London and of travellers passing through on their way to the north.

Reached from the City by the road from Aldersgate and along Goswell Road or via Smithfield and Clerkenwell to St John's Street, it was the starting point for routes leading to St Albans, Lincoln and more distant towns. The roads between London and Islington were very badly maintained and, though short, the journey was not particularly pleasant or easy. In winter they became almost impassable, and travellers often rode across the open fields which were unenclosed and less like quagmires. This way the unwelcome attention of the multitude of aggressive beggars who lay in wait along the 'highways' could generally be avoided. This was a hazard to which even Queen Elizabeth was subjected on one visit to Islington in 1581, as a result of which 74 'begging rogues' were imprisoned in Bridewell.[9] Many of the inns were situated at the southern end of the High Street (Upper Road) and on either side of Islington Green, where there were no fewer than nine on either side of the road in the second half of the century, out of a total 15 'licensed victuallers' for Islington with another three in Holloway, a remarkable number for so small a place. Their names sound familiar today: *The King's Head, The Red Lion, The Bull's Head, The Fleur de Lys* and *The George* among those on the Green. By and large the inns were comfortable, well-run and hospitable, justifying the somewhat eulogistic picture given of them by William Harrison later in the century. Harrison wrote:

> Every man may use his inn as his own house and have for his money how great or little variety of victuals and what other services himself shall think expedient to call for. Our inns are also very well furnished with napery, bedding and tapestry ... Each comer is sure to lie in clean sheets, wherein no man hath been lodged since they came from the laundress ... if the traveller have an horse his bed doth cost him nothing, but if he go on foot he is sure to pay a penny for the same ... If he lose aught while he abideth in the inn, the host is bound by a general custom to restore the damages.[10]

Horses were well looked after by the ostlers, who expected to be well rewarded for their services. But, Harrison warns, some of the servants at the less reputable inns may make extra money by tipping off 'slipper merchants' of the type of baggage travellers were carrying and the route they were following. This could make travel on the major roads leading to the north a hazardous business. Harrison's warning was particularly apt for Islington where the less reputable inns were known to provide a refuge for criminals and fugitives from justice.

Many of the inns were leased by copyholders – virtually secure tenants – from the four Manors, which by the mid-16th century held, both in their original manorial estates and by the acquisition of additional property, much of the land in the parish. Barnesbury Manor had in Norman times covered most of Islington but it had been divided several times since then. By the 16th century the manorial estate included a good portion of the settled area, extending along the central axis of the High Street, the Green and the Upper Street as far as what is now Highbury Cross, with some land in the east round Lower Street (Essex Road) and more to the west round Back Road (now Liverpool Road). The total area of the manorial estate was then 250 acres, equivalent in feudal times to half a knight's fee, but the actual land owned or leased was probably a good deal more.

The mansion occupied by the Fowler family, as Lords of the Manor, was a fine plaster-covered three-storey building on the north side of Cross Street, roughly in the centre of the estate. This was the largest of the four manors in the parish. The other three, Canonbury, Highbury and Prebend (owned by St Paul's and the seat of one of the Prebendaries at the Cathedral) consisted mainly of agricultural land outside the settled area. The houses occupied by the gentry were mostly freehold and there were a number of isolated farmsteads. In the High Street and on the Green were premises occupied by tradesmen practising such crafts as wheelwright, weaver, collar maker, baker, shoemaker, carpenter and tailor.[11]

Thomas Wilkes's inn has not been identified. But various pointers at least make it possible to make a conjecture. From the little that is known of him and from the subsequent lives and connections of members of his family, besides Alice herself, he emerges as a respected member of the Islington community. He was not, as some accounts have suggested, 'a rich landowner', nor was his daughter Alice 'a poor girl'. But he was not just a publican; he was the host of a substantial and reputable inn and he was also a smallholder, being tenant of a meadow of eight acres, called Long Meadow the Greater, from Barnesbury Manor and holding the tenancy of a further 10 acres in the parish. This was all pasture land, used for grazing his cattle and producing hay. His social status was the equivalent of a moderately well-to-do yeoman. He would not have aspired to the rank of 'gentleman' nor would he have been accepted as one. But he would have regarded himself as superior to a mere husbandman or craftsman. Where was his inn? Besides his standing, a clue may lie in the location of his smallholding. Long Meadow the Greater provided the south and west boundary of Highbury Manor, at the north-east end of Barnesbury and his other land may be assumed to have been in the same general area. This points to an inn in Upper Street, further north than the main cluster of inns round the High Street and the Green. A natural choice would be the *King's Head*, in Upper Street opposite St Mary's Church, owned by Barnesbury Manor and the place where the manor courts were held. This immediately stamps it as a superior inn, of a different class from the common or garden type which no doubt characterised those crowded along the High Street, some of which were probably of dubious reputation. It would have been a timber-framed building, two, or perhaps three, storeys high with a first-floor gallery looking over an internal courtyard with stabling for horses at the rear. It might be expected to conform to the standards described by William Harrison. Another contemporary observer elaborates on the sort of hospitality offered at inns of this quality:

> As soon as a passenger comes to an inn, the servants run to him, and one takes his horse, and walks him till he be cold, then rubs him and gives him meat ... Another servant gives the passenger his private chamber and kindles his fire; the third pulls off his boots and makes them clean ... if he will eat at a common table with others his meal will cost him sixpence, yet this course is less honourable and not used by gentlemen. But if he will eat in his chamber, he commands what meat he will.[12]

Many of the inns, and the *King's Head* was surely one, also had post horses for hire charged by the mile. The host and hostess personally supervised the meals for their guests and ensured that they had all they needed. This sounds like the sort of highly respectable inn in which Alice would have been brought up as a child.

St Mary's Church stood in a field on high ground north of Cross Street, just to the east of Upper Street, in the same position as the present church, though in the 16th century it was at the edge of the main settled area. The parsonage house was nearby in Upper Street and the Glebe land amounted to 9½ acres. This provided a valuable supplement to the parson's stipend. Though the Islington living may have been one of the better ones, it has been estimated that in the mid-16th century between one half and three quarters of the parish priests had an annual income of less than £10.[13]

The church, dedicated to St Mary the Virgin, was built in 1483 in the Perpendicular style. It was a 'spacious but low built structure', 92 feet long and 54 feet broad with a tower at the west end 74 feet tall housing six bells. The building was constructed of a mixture of flints, pebbles and chalk, with a tiled roof. Inside the three aisles were paved with brick and stone.[14] Surviving pictures of the old church show the west end almost obscured by the old school house which was built in 1710 and stood close against the church wall. (The old church was demolished as unsafe and a new one built on the same site in 1754; this was destroyed in the Blitz in 1940 and the present church was built in 1956.)

The church played a great part in the lives of the Wilkes family in the 16th and early 17th centuries, being the scene of so many of their Christian rites of passage. The registers are sadly deficient; none exist before 1558 and thereafter they are incomplete. But there is no doubt that all six Wilkes children were baptised at St Mary's. Thomas Wilkes was buried there, as certainly were both his wives. Margery and Robert, his two elder children, were both married and buried at St Mary's. Alice celebrated her second marriage, to William Elkin, at the church, where she and her only surviving son, Henry Robinson, were buried. So also were Christopher Wilkes and his children and Margery's eldest son, Thomas. These are the known family connections; there were no doubt others which have gone unrecorded. And several of those who returned to

St Mary's as their final resting place had, like Alice, spent their adult lives away from Islington.

It was not just for these rites of passage, nor even just for the Sunday services, that the Wilkes family and their neighbours attended St Mary's. In Islington, as elsewhere in the country, in towns as well as in villages, the parish church was, as it had been in medieval England, the centre of social life, even more than the inn. In this the Catholic early part of the 16th century was no different from the later Protestant part, though the rigours of Edwardian Protestantism put something of a temporary damper on the traditional activities. Most people in Henry's reign regularly attended the Mass in Latin, which they could not understand and in which they played little part, because they believed this and the other disciplines imposed by the Catholic faith were necessary for salvation. Most of the same people, some no doubt suppressing their conscientious scruples, other than those who were prepared to risk the penalties of the law by absenting themselves, turned out on Sunday for Morning Prayer in English established by the prayer books of Edward and Elizabeth. At least they could understand the service and had the benefit of being able to hear the original words of the scriptures read in their own language instead of having to rely on the selective interpretation of the Catholic priest. The church was also the place where people met to exchange news and gossip, and the centre of colourful events which, besides their religious significance, provided a major source of entertainment in contrast to the drabness and grinding hard work of most ordinary people's lives. Christmas festivities, the dramatic period of the Passiontide followed by the joyous celebration of Easter, Corpus Christi processions were all severely tempered by the Protestant reforms and the number of annual religious feast days was reduced, according to William Harrison, from 95 to 27 as well as the elimination of 30 celebrations of the eves of saints days. But even these religious festivities could not be entirely suppressed and such traditional events as Mayday dancing, the Whitsuntide 'Church ale' – to raise funds for the church – and the Harvest Festival celebrations continued as well as some more personal activities such as 'Bride ales' and other excuses for a good party.

In terms of religious practice the period of Alice's childhood was uncomfortable and confusing for the ordinary members of the village congregation. The strict enforcement of Protestant legislation described in the preceding chapter must have been difficult enough to accept. But special resentment was caused when the much-loved image of 'Our Lady of Islington' was removed from the church and publicly burned on Islington Green. During these six years of dramatic changes some of the inns acquired a reputation as meeting places for Catholic recusants, who, whether they were penalised or not, were able to return to what they hoped would be the reinstatement in the church of the true religion during Queen Mary's reign. Little did they know how soon their hopes, which were shared secretly by many of the regular law-abiding parishioners who had only with difficulty brought themselves to accept the changes, were to be dashed.

In Islington, as elsewhere, there were instances of active resistance to the Catholic restoration. In 1557 a Protestant preacher, John Rough, an associate of John Knox, was arrested at the *Saracen's Head* inn where a congregation had assembled to pray and read the English Bible, using Cranmer's Prayer Book. He and others were brought for trial before Bishop Bonner of London, who condemned them to be burned at the stake. Rough was burned at Smithfield and four others, all together, near the church in Islington on 15 September.[15] In June of the following year, 40 people were arrested in a field in the village where they were holding a Protestant service; some escaped but 22 were tried and convicted of heresy, all having refused to recant. In all 13 were burned; the remainder either died in prison or escaped. One specially recalcitrant young man was taken by Bishop Bonner to his own palace, placed over night in stocks and on the following day beaten personally by the Bishop with two willow rods in the presence of two robed priests.[16] These were among the last of the Protestant men and women who were burned at the stake for heresy during the five years of Queen Mary's reign. In Elizabeth's reign relative calm appears to have prevailed in Islington apart from some cases of fines imposed on Catholic recusants for failure to attend Anglican services at St Mary's.

The radical reforms and counter-reforms, both physical and doctrinal, were particularly hard on a conscientious parish priest. James Robinson, appointed vicar of St Mary's in 1545, was evidently unable to take the iconoclasm of Edwardian Protestantism. He resigned in 1550, no doubt finding Cranmer's first prayer book the last straw. His successor, William Jennins, was more resilient and more flexible. Though his arrival followed immediately on the abolition of the celibacy requirement, it is not known that he was married; if he was, he managed to conceal the fact or he would have been in trouble in Mary's reign. On his appointment he was committed to the Protestant reforms, but he managed to survive the short-lived Catholic restoration and remained at St Mary's until 1565 by which time the Church of England was firmly by law established. He then moved on to St Pancras in Soper Lane, a well-established Protestant church in the City.

There is nothing to show where the religious sympathies of the Wilkes family lay during this period. That Thomas and his children fulfilled their obligation to attend church regularly on Sundays and other Holy Days can be assumed. Thomas himself, born well before the Reformation, was certainly brought up to accept the full sacramental doctrine of the Catholic faith. But his elder children, Margery and Robert, were aged about ten and seven respectively by 1550 and all their early religious instruction would have been at services conducted and of scriptures read in English, in which Alice was soon to join them. So the reintroduction of Latin and the Catholic Mass, in a language they did not understand, must have been distressing. Where did their father stand? For him it must have appeared as the restoration of the old religion he knew, after a short unwelcome break. No-one, of course, realised how short-lived the restoration was to be, but the incidents related above show at least that Queen Mary's attempt to bring back the Pope, combined it must be said with the unpopularity of her Spanish marriage, struck a strong level of resistance and revealed a hard core of support for Protestantism in Islington. One can imagine that, as a devout and conscientious father, Thomas continued to read the Bible in English and perhaps even the Collects to his family in the privacy of their home while insisting they attended Catholic Mass on Sunday.

Thomas did not live to see the end of the Catholic interlude but his children did. When the English Prayer Book and Bible were brought back in 1559, Alice was fortunate in having the same parish priest of Protestant convictions throughout the remainder of her childhood and adolescence. It is easy to assume that William Jennins conscientiously performed his pastoral duties in conformity with the prevailing doctrine, though it must be admitted that there is no evidence on this point one way or the other. But it was the Protestant Anglican doctrine implanted at this formative period of Alice's life which was to provide the motivation for the Christian acts of charity which are associated with her memory.

There is no extant information about the early education of Alice and her older siblings. Prior to the abolition of the chantries in 1547 as encouraging 'superstition and error', primary education was often given to young children by local chantry priests. Although there was no formal system of education for girls, they were often admitted to these 'petty' schools along with boys from the age of five. So Margery may have learned to read (though not to write) at a chantry school. And there are plenty of indications that this form of elementary education was continued generally throughout the country following the demise of the chantries. It was indeed an essential preparation for boys planning to enter one of the growing number of grammar schools or to embark on a craft apprenticeship. Rich families were able to provide this education by employing chaplains or, by the middle of the century, private schoolmasters. But for middle-class boys the need was often supplied by the parish priest, who welcomed the opportunity to supplement his meagre stipend, or even by the churchwardens. Robert's basic education will have taken place at a class of this kind, but he will also, from an early age, have learned much about the business of innkeeping and about husbandry from his father.

Alice was clearly a lively, intelligent and probably rather precocious little girl. Like her sister, she will have been encouraged by her father to read. Having lost her mother at a very early age and with a stepmother heavily occupied with the care of three children besides her household duties, Alice may be expected to have grown up quickly, to have taken a share in the work of the house and no doubt to have learned soon how to use her considerable charm. One can imagine that she was popular with the patrons of her father's inn, among whom were included members of the local gentry, and that her wider education benefited from these contacts which may indeed have sown seeds of ambition for her own future.

Early in Alice's life occurred the event which led in due course to the creation of her great life's work and lasting memorial. This was the incident of the arrow and the hat. There are several versions of this story and alternative suggestions for the date when it took place. Some of the versions contain embellishments which are wide of the mark. But the location where the incident took place is common to almost all. This was the open ground and fields between London and Islington which had been since the 15th century devoted to the practice of archery. For many years the Artillery Company, a body of men armed with long-bows, had had the right to march through Finsbury Field towards Islington and to break down gates and fences which obstructed their route. In 1538 Henry VIII established the Fraternity of St George with licence to practise shooting with the long-bow in Clerkenwell Field, where they were permitted to set up a series of wooden and stone targets, numbering 160 in all, of different heights and at distances from one another varying from 180 to 400 yards. The fraternity had the right to demolish any obstacles which obscured the vision of any target from the one next before it. Moreover, an indemnity was granted to any member of the Fraternity who, having shouted 'Fast', happened, with an arrow from his long-bow, to harm or even kill anyone passing between the archer and his target![17] This practice, which declined in the latter part of the century, must have made the countryside south of Clerkenwell a hazardous place for casual walkers or people wishing to pursue other recreational activities. The villagers of Islington and Clerkenwell did nevertheless graze their cattle in fields on the outskirts of the villages and no doubt pushed their luck by gradually extending the grazing area.

It was in these fields that, early in Alice's life, there occurred the famous incident of the arrow which was to lead ultimately to her decision to build the almshouses and school which bore her name. Only five years after her death the incident is described in John Stow's *Survey of London* in the following terms:

> This worthy woman, being born at Islington, in the time of her childhood, she happened there to escape a great danger, by means of an arrow shot at random in the field, where she was then sporting among other children. The arrow missing all the other, pierced quite through the hat on her head, and (God be praised for it) did not touch her with any other harm: whereupon, in the town of her birth, and where she escaped such an [un]expected peril, she made choice to express her thankfulness to God upon the altar of her charitable almshouses and school.[18]

The traditional account is more detailed and contains some points not included in the version given by Stow. This account was recorded in a work published at the beginning of the 19th century and was also included in identical terms in two histories of Islington published later in the century. The authors claimed that it was 'extracted from a record belonging to the Brewers' Company'. One of them states that it appeared in a book published towards the end of the 17th century. Unfortunately no trace of the original record has been found in the Company's archives. But there is no reason to doubt the claims of the authors or indeed the authenticity of the record quoted.[19] The account reads as follows:

> In the reign of Queen Mary it was an exercise for archers to shoot with their bows and arrows at butts; this part of Islington at that time being all open fields and pasture land; and on the same spot of ground where the school now stands, was a woman milking a cow. The Lady Owen, then a maiden gentlewoman, walking by with her maid-servant, observed the woman a milking, and had a mind to try the cow's paps, whether she could milk, which she did, and at her withdrawing from the cow, an arrow was shot through the crown of her hat (at which time high-crowned hats were in fashion) which so startled her that she then declared, that if she lived to be a Lady she would erect something on that very spot of ground, in commemoration of the great mercy shown by the Almighty in that astonishing deliverance. This passed on until she became a widow lady; her servant at the time this accident happened, being still living with her Lady, reminded her Lady of her former words. Her answer was she remembered the affair, and would fulfil her promise.[20]

It is not easy to fix the date of this episode. One suggestion is that it took place in 1562 when Alice was fifteen.[21] Certainly by the standards of the time she was by then a young woman, of an age when many girls got married, and might be described as a 'maiden gentlewoman', though the title probably reflects the status she had acquired by the time of her death rather than her rank as an innkeeper's daughter at the time of the incident. But the reference to Queen Mary's reign, if taken literally, implies that the year was 1558 at the latest, when Alice would have been eleven. In those days, and given her upbringing, she would have been quite capable of milking a cow. She was, after all, only one year short of the 'age of consent' when she would legally be entitled to marry without her parents' permission. The maid-servant was probably a slightly older village girl, say about sixteen, employed by her father to look after Alice; given that the girl remained with Alice for the rest of her life, she may have been the Ann Powell who received a legacy in Alice's Will. Such slender evidence as there is – and it must be admitted that there can be no certainty about this – seems to point to 1558 as the date of the episode.

Thomas Wilkes died sometime in 1558. He was buried, according to his wish, at St Mary's but no date was recorded. He made his Will on 18 February and probate was granted on 21 May, so his death probably took place in April or early May. He provided for his widow Margaret and her three children and left legacies in money and in kind to Margery and Alice. His bequests to Robert, aged fifteen or sixteen by then, included his gray mare, a bull calf, a heffer in calf, a crop of hay, his farm cart and his clothes! Robert Wood of Islington who, together with Thomas himself and his wife, Margaret, was a signatory of the Will, was made Alice's guardian until her coming of age or marriage, which must have been a great relief to the widow. Clearly he was a close friend of the family but what part he played in Alice's life is not known. He is almost certainly the Robert Wood who died in April 1593 and was buried at St James's, Clerkenwell; his short Will, drawn up and signed on 7 April on his behalf, as he was too ill to do it himself, describes him as a 'gentleman' of Islington and contains bequests to his family of his property in the parish. By that time Alice was married to her second husband, so Robert Wood had long since ceased to have any responsibility for her.

On 23 April 1559 Margery Wilkes married John Draper at St Mary's. John was a London brewer whose business was established in the Whitefriars area, south of Fleet Street, near the site of the former Carmelite monastery dissolved by Henry VIII, and who had a house in Chancery Lane as well as one in Islington. There is no record of Alice's life in the years immediately following her father's death. She may have remained with her stepmother and the young children for a year or two. But it is likely that at least from the early 1560s she spent much of her time with her sister and brother-in-law. She would have been a great help to Margery when her children began to arrive and her acquaintance with the brewing community would provide an obvious introduction to the next phase in her life.

Chapter 3

Brewers All

Whether or not Thomas Wilkes was, or was entitled to be, a member of the Worshipful Company of Innholders is not known. By calling himself 'Innholder' he claimed a status, first recognised by the City authorities in 1473, superior to that of 'Hosteler' or 'Herbergeour'. But that he was not a Freeman of the Company is clear, or he would have said so in his Will. The Company's first Charter, granted by Henry VIII in 1515, applied to the City of London, but this would not necessarily have precluded the admission of respectable innkeepers from the neighbouring villages, especially one such as Islington where so many inns were located. Most of the early records of the Company were destroyed in the Great Fire of 1666, but the range of the second Charter granted by Charles II in 1663, which has survived, extended beyond the boundaries of the City wall. Considering the status of many of Thomas's patrons, however, it can be taken for granted that the conditions and standards he was required to observe in order to qualify for his licence were comparable to those applied by the Company to inns in the City.

Thomas will have maintained a well-stocked cellar, providing ale of various strengths and a quantity of imported wines. The popularity of the latter grew during the 16th century and the gentry frequented wine-taverns and the better class of inn where they could rely on finding a greater choice of good quality wines than all except the very rich were able to afford to keep in their own homes. At this time no wine was produced in England. William Harrison, writing in the second half of the century, reports that 56 varieties of light red and white wines were imported from France and some 30 types of heavier wines from Italy, Spain and Greece. Ale was still, as it had been for centuries, the staple drink of English people of all classes. Food to go with it varied from the exotic and luxurious to the very simple. But meat and bread – for the rich made of wheat and for the poor of rye – formed the constant basis of most people's diet; for the very poor indeed bread alone, sometimes even made from beans or lentils and oats, had to suffice.

The prevalence of ale as the universal drink throughout the country was largely due to the risk of drinking water, especially in towns and villages, where it was drawn from communal wells or open conduits. There was no means of ensuring that these sources were free from contamination and serious illness and death could result from drinking water from them. The brewing process had a sterilising effect. Prior to the 16th century the brewing of ale was mainly a domestic business, each ale-house producing enough to meet its own requirements. Because ale was such an essential commodity its price and quality were from an early date strictly regulated with penalties for infringement which were frequently applied against offenders. Through these malpractices and the widespread drunkenness which hosts (and hostesses) either could not or did not try to restrain, alehouses gained an unsavoury reputation in the 14th and 15th centuries. This brought the ale brewers into frequent conflict with the City of London authorities at this period. The relationship began to improve after the Brewers' Gild became an incorporated Company on the grant of a Royal Charter by Henry VI in 1437. As a result the Company acquired the right to exercise control over those involved in the trade in the City and to make rules designed to stamp out the dishonest practices. This was not easy and not invariably successful. The Company was again in trouble with the City authorities in the mid-16th century as described below.

By the second half of the 15th century the City Companies were playing a major part in the government of the City, and it was established that a citizen could only become a Freeman of the City of London (which carried certain privileges such as freedom from impressment into the army) through membership of a recognised Livery Company. The importance of the Brewers' Company lay not so much in its members' wealth – in this respect they could not compare with the Mercers, Goldsmiths and some others – but in the universality of its product. In the order of precedence among City Companies established in 1516 the Brewers were not ranked among the wealthiest 'Great Twelve', from which the Lord Mayor of London was almost always chosen, but were accorded 14th place, which they retain today.[1]

The connection of the Wilkes family with brewing was close. It has already been related that Thomas's elder daughter, Margery, married a brewer, John Draper, in 1559. Thomas's son, Robert, lived and died a brewer in Islington. And, most important, Alice's first husband, Henry Robinson, whose story will be told shortly, was also a brewer.

Two major developments in the late 15th and early 16th centuries affected the brewing industry and thus the opportunities for Thomas Wilkes's descendants who were involved in the brewing trade. One was the introduction of wholesale brewing. Large-scale brewing, prior to the 16th century, was mainly confined to the monasteries. The quantity of ale consumed by the monks was not small; the daily allowance for each monk at the Abbey of St Edmundsbury, for example, was one gallon. Besides this, the abbeys often provided weak ale to travellers who lodged with them for the night. But this came to an end with the dissolution of the monasteries in the 1530s.

Otherwise, as indicated above, brewing was essentially a domestic industry linked to a single retail outlet, often managed by an ale-wife. The number of small brew-houses in the City of London proliferated to such an extent that, by the end of the 14th century, there was approximately one to every 12 inhabitants.[2] Gradually the custom grew for owners of small ale houses, who were not members of the Brewers' Company, and the inn and tavern keepers, many of whom probably were members, to buy their supplies from the larger brewers. By the early 16th century this practice led to the establishment of a profitable wholesale industry. The wholesalers produced ale of different strengths to meet their customers' requirements and were able to store it for the time necessary to bring it to maturity. According to William Harrison ale was best brewed in March and kept for a year before drinking, though the brewers' desire for a quick profit makes it unlikely that this ideal was always observed. Harrison's comment that the water of the River Thames was considered excellent for brewing (polluted though it must have been) may do no more than reflect the fact that many breweries were located near to its banks, for the obvious reason that the principal requirement of the brewing process was a ready supply of water.

It was in the brewhouses that they established in the City that John Draper and Henry Robinson were in due course to make the fortunes which they were able to pass on to their families. John's brewery was in the Whitefriars district, in the precincts of the former Dominican and Carmelite priories; Henry's was in Blackfriars. Both were conveniently near to the Thames, not only a source of water but also used as a means of transportation. But this was still well in the future. At the time of Thomas Wilkes's death in 1559, Henry had not even started his apprenticeship. John had not reached the age for admission to the Freedom of the Company, which was set in 1555 at 24,[3] and it was a further nine years before he became master of his first apprentice. Unlike his brothers-in-law, Robert Wilkes, who remained in Islington trading as a 'beere-brewer', did not qualify for the Freedom of the City. His brewery may possibly have been located in Hopping Lane, which then ran between Upper Street at the northern limit of the main settled area and Lower Street (Essex Road) and the origin of which probably dates from the period when 'hopping beer' was becoming popular (see below). (Hopping Lane survives today as a minor cul-de-sac in Canonbury.)

The other development was the introduction of hops into England in the 15th century. These were brought into the country and used in brewing by immigrants, mainly from Flanders and Holland, who set up their breweries on the South Bank of the Thames in Southwark (which was until 1550 outside the City and the jurisdiction of the Brewers' Company). For hundreds of years ale had been brewed from barley, grown principally in East Anglia, which was converted, by a process of soaking in water and then roasting, into malt; the malt was then ground and mashed in water, and finally fermented with yeast, known to medieval brewers as 'godisgood'. Competition from these upstart foreign traders and their 'hopping beer' was strongly resisted by the London brewers, who were successful in getting the use of hops in brewing banned under Edward IV. However, by the end of the 15th century the ban had been lifted and the beer-brewers had established a Gild of their own, separate from the Brewers' Company. Henry VIII proved more sympathetic to the brewers' complaints and reimposed the ban. Besides the commercial grounds for the ban, the case against hops on grounds of health was put by Andrew Boorde in his *Dietary of Health* in 1542:

> Ale for an Englishman is a natural drinke. Beer is made of malt, of hoppes and water; it is the naturall drynke for a Dutch man, and now of late dayes is much used in England to the detryment of many English people, specyally it kylleth them the which be troubled with the colyke; and the stone and the strangulation; for the drynke is a colde drinke, yet it doth make a man fat and doth inflate the bely, as it doth appear by the Dutch men's faces and belyes.[4]

A prescient warning of the perils of over-indulgence in 'hopping beet'; today's 'beer belly' has a long history!

Henry VIII's ban did not outlast his successor. Ale, as traditionally brewed, had a relatively short life and the English brewers had begun to realise the value of hops as a preservative and to accept that it was no longer in their interest to resist this foreign intrusion. So in 1552 Edward VI passed legislation permitting the use of hops by English brewers;[5] a few years later a further Act brought the beer-brewers within the control of the Brewers' Company. These measures were followed by two new Charters granted by Queen Elizabeth which extended the jurisdiction of the Company to include Southwark, where many of the foreign brew-houses making hopping beer had set up in business and where also were to be found some of the disreputable ale-houses. The same extension also brought most of Islington within the area subject to the Company's regulation. As the public taste for hopping beer grew, the distinction between ale and beer ceased to be significant and the practice of using hops in brewing was generally adopted. John Draper and Henry Robinson made their beer with barley from East Anglia and hops from Kent.

Though the Company derived its privileges from its Royal Charters, the Mayor and Aldermen were responsible for the regulation of trade in the City. So the ordinances which gave the Company power to exercise control over the industry were issued by the City authorities. These gave the Brewers' Company the duty to enforce regulations on price and quality of ale and beer brewed in the City and on the measures and vessels in which it was sold to the public. By the time the Draper, Robinson and Wilkes families were becoming involved in the brewing business, these powers were well established. Prior to the middle of the 16th century the Company was under the control of the Wardens, usually four in number. From 1563 onwards it became the practice to elect annually a single Master of the Brewers' Company who served for one year. He was assisted by three Wardens also elected annually, and by a Court of Assistants consisting of senior members of the Company, all of whom had usually already held office as Master or Warden; together they had the task of enforcing the regulations. The Master and Wardens attended the Common Council of the City of London, of which membership was restricted to Liverymen of the City Companies.[6]

The Brewers were not always very efficient, or indeed very rigorous, at carrying out their responsibilities. It was much more profitable to sell double (or strong) beer than weaker ('small') beer, which was cheaper, so that the growing popular demand for the latter, as the staple drink at all times of day, was often not met, and, when it was, the quality was often below standard. The result was a shortage of supplies to the ale-houses and consequent over-charging and dilution. This brought the Brewers again into conflict with the City authorities and in 1551 their representatives were temporarily banished from the Common Council. At the same time the Mayor and Aldermen appointed four Surveyors of Beer to reinforce the traditional 'Aleconners',[7] whose purpose was to 'assist' the Company in the exercise of its duties, in other words to make sure the Company was applying the regulations strictly and fairly. The continuing need for what was in effect an arrangement for monitoring the Company's activities was demonstrated by the order which the Mayor was constrained to give in 1597 that 52 barrels of beer 'being neither fit for man's body nor to be converted into sawce shall have the heads of all the same beaten out, and the beer poured into the channells, part in Cheapside, part in Cornhill and part in Bishopsgate.'[8]

Admission to the Brewers' Company, as to any other of the 60 Livery Companies of the City of London, followed completion of an apprenticeship. This has its origins in the rules of the medieval craft guilds, which by the end of the 15th century had become incorporated by Royal Charter, for the training of boys, and in some cases girls, in the 'misteries of the trade'. In the first part of the 16th century individual Companies ran their own schemes. John Draper served his apprenticeship during this period and John Robinson began his. Then in 1563 the 'Statute of Artificers' was introduced which gave the force of law to a unified system throughout the country incorporating most of the traditional arrangements and in the City of London leaving their administration to the Companies. For the children of paupers service as an apprentice, usually in one of the less profitable occupations, was compulsory by order of the local justices, payment to masters being a charge on the parish. For the 'non-poor' apprenticeship provided an alternative to university or the law for the training and discipline of teenage youths, which equipped them with skills to make them capable, in theory and often in practice, of earning their living for the next thirty years or more. The Drapers, Robinsons and, as will be seen later, the Elkins, belonged to this class.[9]

Apprentices normally started at the age of fourteen or fifteen and served for seven years. Masters (not to be confused with the annually elected Master of the Brewers' Company) were master craftsmen of the Brewers' Company who had set up in business and had the approval of the Wardens to take on apprentices, to the limit of no more than three at one time. For the non-poor the master and the boy's father were obliged to sign a written indenture defining the terms of service. This was accompanied by the payment of a premium, the amount of which was not fixed but could be of the order of £50 in London. The apprentice lived in the master's house as one of the family, the master being in effect in *loco parentis*. So the choice of master was a matter of great importance for the boy's parents. Often boys were apprenticed to a relative or family friend, as seems to have been the case with some of the Drapers and Robinsons.

Apprentices were under strict discipline and expected to work hard. While hours of work varied, a 12-hour day from 7a.m. to 7p.m. was common and in many cases this was extended to 14 hours in summer, for six days in the week. Holidays were short and scarce, normally restricted to Christmas and Easter, Mothering Sunday, May Day, various Church festivals and especially Shrove Tuesday which was traditionally a day for celebration by apprentices. Many leisure activities indulged in by adults were forbidden to apprentices. They were not allowed to enter taverns and ale-houses, or to play at cards and dice, or to gamble. And, during their apprenticeship they must not contract matrimony or 'commit fornication' (though the latter for some reason does not appear to have been forbidden in paupers' contracts!). Other forbidden activities, according to the individual indenture, could include tennis, bowling, cockfighting and even dancing, though some of these were relaxed on Shrove Tuesday. Above all they were bound to serve their master faithfully, obey his lawful commands and, most important in the special interests of the craft as well as those of the master, keep their master's secrets.

Masters were entitled to administer 'moderate' punishment for infringements but could not summarily dismiss an apprentice for misconduct. Short absences, minor theft or occasional drunkenness were not regarded as serious offences. More serious ones, or habitual misdemeanours, would be referred to the Court of Assistants, who might order the offender to be whipped. If a criminal breach of the law was committed, the apprentice would, like any other citizen, be brought before the magistrates.

This was a pretty tough regime with little leisure or permitted amusements. A tendency to rowdiness and indiscipline on the part of teenage boys so restricted was only to be expected. 'Apprentices' acquired a reputation for bad behaviour in the 16th century rather akin to 'students' in the 21st. This was unfair to the many apprentices, especially in the quality trades, who worked hard to justify their fathers' investment in their future. But not infrequently bad and oppressive masters were the cause of bad behaviour by apprentices, especially when it resulted in exploitation of boys from poorer homes. Such occurrences must have been rare in the Brewers' Company, in which the apprentices were not only governed by indentures negotiated with their fathers but also required the approval of the Wardens before starting their service.[10]

For their part, masters accepted certain obligations besides imparting instruction in the skills of their trade. Bed and board were provided and all necessary clothes. As regards the latter, apprentices wore a standard uniform of blue gowns, flat top caps and shiny shoes and the only weapon permitted was a pocket knife! Often, also, masters arranged for the apprentice to be educated in reading, writing and counting and undertook to supply religious and social training, the former certainly involving attendance at church on Sunday.

Altogether it may sound as though the apprentice had a fairly joyless life. But of course all the rules were not strictly enforced; everything depended on the attitude of the master, and, no less important, of his wife. In the best situations, the apprentice became fully integrated into the family, especially in cases where the master or his wife was a relative or friend of the family. There are many instances of apprentices marrying their master's daughter, an outcome which was encouraged by the lack of opportunity for contact with the opposite sex. In many cases an apprentice who had learned his master's craft thoroughly by diligent application over a period of seven years would be likely to prove a valuable partner for his master and, where there was no son available to take over, a potential inheritor of the business. Such a man would be a good match for the master's daughter.

On completion of their apprenticeship in the Brewers' Company, newly qualified apprentices had to be presented to the Wardens by their master and 'no apprentice who has served his term shall become a Chief Brewer or Under Brewer, and therefore take wages, until certified as able by the said Wardens under penalty prescribed.' This applied to those apprentices who became 'journeymen', that is employees of a master brewer, and did not intend, or could not afford, to advance to the Freedom of the Brewers' Company, and thus of the City.[11]

Those who wished to become Freemen had also to appear before the Wardens, but an apprentice could not be admitted to the Freedom or set up in business until the age of twenty-four. There were four methods of acquiring the status of Freeman, and thus an apprentice master. The first was by patrimony, that is to say inheritance of the status, a route which was available to all lineal descendants of an existing Freeman of the Company. This method applied to the sons and grandsons of John Draper, and possibly even to John himself. The second, already mentioned above, was marriage to the master's daughter, a not infrequent occurrence which, so far as the apprentice was concerned, was usually cost-free. A variation of this method was for an apprentice to marry his master's widow. As will be seen later, William Elkin, a mercer who became Alice's second husband, benefited from this.

The third option was for the apprentice either to buy a partnership with his own or another master or to set up on his own account. The former might not cost much if the master took a liking to the apprentice and was glad to take him on as a junior partner, possibly on payment of a small premium. But the latter could be expensive if it meant establishing a new business or buying an existing one. At a much later period – the first half of the 18th century – the cost of setting up for a brewer has been estimated as a minimum of £2,000 and probably a good deal more, one of the most expensive trades at that period. Even in the 16th century the father of an apprentice wishing to set up on his own must have had to find a considerable sum. Henry Robinson adopted the third option and in due course set up on his own. Finally, there was the possibility of obtaining the privilege of freedom of a Livery Company by redemption, that is by straight purchase. Those who were admitted in this way did not necessarily engage in the trade, and the option was more likely to be adopted by someone aspiring to hold one of the major offices in the City which were in practice only open to Freemen of the 'Big Twelve' Companies, among which the Brewers' Company, at number 14, did not feature. Senior Freemen of the Company were, by selection of the Master, Wardens and Court of Assistants, placed 'on the livery'. This honour involved a good deal of expense as they had to buy their own liveries, gowns and hoods, and replace them with new ones every three years; the colour of the gown was regularly changed and that of the hood was the gown colour and red.[12] The illustration is of a portrait of Alderman Richard Platt who was twice Master of the Brewers' Company and was the founder in 1595 of Aldenham School which was administered as a charitable trust by the Brewers'; he is not wearing the Company's livery.

John Draper was a Freeman of the Brewers' Company and a Citizen of the City of London. He clearly became prosperous in his business, though he never held high office in the City or the Company. He took on four apprentices between 1568 and 1573, who learned their craft at his brewhouse in Whitefriars, situated between Fleet Street and the Thames. In 1572 he was appointed a Governor of Highgate School, which was founded in 1565 by the then Lord Chancellor to provide free education to 40 poor children of Highgate. John died in 1576, leaving properties in the City, Hornsey, Clerkenwell and elsewhere, and residences in Ludgate (Blackfriars) and in the Islington hamlet of Stroud Green. These were divided among his wife and his five sons and his daughter. Among other bequests were one to his 'good neighbours in the parish of St Dunstan in the West, Fleet Street' and, to the Brewers' Company, the lease of a tenement in the Barbican. His wife, Margery, exercised her right as a widow to assume her husband's status as a master, and took on an apprentice in 1580. She probably retained this status until her eldest son, Thomas, who was born in 1564, reached the age at which he could take over.

The Draper family provided a succession of brewers. John's father, Thomas, may have been a member of the Brewers' Company; he was instrumental in arranging the lease to John of an inn in Billingsgate in 1574. Two certainly, and possibly three of John's sons became brewers. Thomas, who took on 11 apprentices between 1585 and 1611, was a Warden in 1590 and Master of the Brewers' Company in 1602. Henry, with 16 apprentices between 1587 and 1613, was twice a Warden and Master in 1606 and again in 1608. Jasper may also have been a Freeman of the Company.[13] In the next generation, Thomas's son Robert was a Warden in 1627 and Master in 1637.

Alice's first husband, Henry Robinson, was one of two 'supervisors' of his brother-in-law, John Draper's Will. Henry took on 14 apprentices between 1569 and 1585 and held the appointment of Warden in 1580. His story is told in the next chapter. The other 'supervisor' was Alice's brother, Robert Wilkes. He took on three apprentices between 1577 and 1583, one of whom was his nephew, Henry Draper. He was a Warden in 1583 and in 1590; after his death in 1598 his widow, Judith, also appears to have taken on two apprentices, in 1600 and 1608, the first being taken over from Thomas Draper.

The above account shows not only the close connections of the three families with the Brewers' Company but also the strong ties which existed between them. With this background it is not hard to understand why Alice chose the Brewers' Company as the trustees of the foundation she established towards the end of her life.

Chapter 4

Elizabethan London

Alice never abandoned her roots in Islington, which was to become the location of the foundation for which she is remembered today. She became a Londoner by adoption since she lived most of her life in the City and all her three husbands were Citizens of London. She moved there in 1570 at the age of 23 on her first marriage. As already suggested, it is possible that she had spent some time in London earlier in the 1560s staying with her married elder sister.

The City of London was the mercantile and industrial capital of England, far outstripping any other town in size and wealth. It was effectively governed by the great merchant companies whose importance as providers of funds for the Crown and Government gave them power and influence which could not be ignored. This, combined with the City's long-established privileges and customs, gave it a semi-independent status which was grudgingly accepted by, but often a source of friction with, the government at Westminster. Alice's first two husbands Henry Robinson and William Elkin were Freemen respectively of the Brewers' and Mercers' companies and both lived and amassed their fortunes in the City. Her third husband Thomas Owen lived in the City and was to be granted the honorary Freedom of the Mercers' Company.

The core of the City comprised the square mile enclosed within the wall to which was added as much again outside it. The wall started from the Tower, a Royal Palace, in the east and following the line of the old Roman wall, took a wide sweep round the north via Bishopsgate and the present 'London Wall'. It ran down the east bank of the Fleet River (now underground) to reach the Thames a little to the west of the present Blackfriars Bridge. Its total length was just over two miles.[1] The wall was surrounded by a ditch much of which was choked with rubbish despite periodic attempts by the City authorities to clear it. The southern boundary of the City within the wall was formed by the River Thames.

The City was divided into 26 electoral wards. Twenty lay wholly within the wall, three straddled it to the north, and three were wholly outside: one to the east of the Tower; one to the west on the north and south side of Fleet Street; and the third, added in 1550, on the south bank of the river in Southwark. The wards were the constituencies from which leading merchants were elected as Aldermen in the City's Government. They remain virtually unchanged today.[2] The wall was punctuated by seven principal gates, the names of which are preserved in present day streets, attached to substantial buildings in the wall, and three small postern gates.[3] The gates, on top of which the authorities had a nasty habit of displaying the heads and limbs of executed criminals, were all closed at night from dusk to dawn, which sounds inconvenient until one realises that the absence of lighting made it difficult for people to move about at night on legitimate business outside their homes. In any case within the wall the curfew, signalled by the ringing of church bells when the gates were closed, was in theory enforced by the Constable and the Watch with his staff and lantern. Richer citizens who could afford to employ servants to carry torches no doubt found ways of circumventing these restrictions on their nocturnal social life.[4]

Access to the river was by numerous 'stairs' and quays along the banks where the wherries (simple rowboats with one or two oarsmen each) manned by Watermen waited for hire as water taxis. They not only ferried passengers across the river but were the most convenient form of transport from one end of the City to the other and on to Westminster in the west, thus avoiding the crowded City streets. The river was a much used highway. Besides the two thousand wherries, which gave employment to three thousand men, there were the larger tiltboats which carried up to ten people sheltered by a canopy and the great barges of the City companies, highly decorated with comfortable seats for passengers and driven by a dozen or more pairs of oars.[5] The only bridge across the Thames in Elizabeth's time (and indeed until the 18th century) was London Bridge, a very different structure from its successor today. It was built on 20 stone arches, which created dangerous turbulence as the river forced its way through the openings which were narrowed by silt and debris, so prudent travellers bypassed the bridge on foot. Along each side of the bridge were houses of rich merchants, and shops selling a variety of merchandise, whose owners lived above. It was the main way into the City from the south, used by carts bringing supplies of food and building materials, flocks of sheep and herds of cattle as well as pedestrians. Visitors approaching the City by this route were faced with the gruesome spectacle of the heads of people executed for treason displayed on top of the tower of the drawbridge which was no longer used.[6]

The population of the City within and without the wall when Alice first arrived there has been estimated as about 80,000, representing just under three per cent of the total population of England.[7] It included a small number of foreigners, mainly Protestant refugees from the Continent whose business activities were a greater irritant to the indigenous merchant community than their number warranted.[8] By the end of the century the population of the City had increased by more than fifty per cent. This was achieved despite the vast death toll from the plague and other diseases and reflected the inexorable growth of London as the centre of commerce and international trade.[9] A less welcome addition was the influx of unemployed, landless labourers from the country who came to seek work or beg in the City and thus swelled the existing and ubiquitous ranks of London's poor.

The official boundaries of the City and thus of the Lord Mayor's jurisdiction were marked by 'bars' at some distance outside the gates.[10] The best known of these is Temple Bar at the western end of Fleet Street which marked the outer limit of the westernmost ward. This was the point at which by long-standing custom the Sovereign halted and sought the Lord Mayor's permission to enter his domain, after sending the Royal Herald ahead to knock on the Ludgate, which was closed on the Sovereign's approach.[11] Beyond the bars to the north and north-west of the City were the suburbs with many fine brick-built houses as well as historic mansions along the main routes to the north of the country, and with tenements for the poor situated mainly in the side streets. Increasingly also the noisier and dirtier industries, such as gun foundries and brick kilns, were established in the suburbs, which were expanding faster as areas of residential and industrial development than the overcrowded City itself. This sprawling ribbon development encroached on the open countryside. The latter at some points still ran almost to the City wall, identified by such familiar names as Spitalfield, Moorfield, Smithfield and Finsburyfield.

Beyond Temple Bar to the west was the Strand, lined on its south side with great mansions built by the rich and powerful as their London residences with gardens running down to the river – Essex House, Arundel House, Somerset House, the Savoy and Bedford House. This was the highway, a little less than a mile long, to Westminster, the seat of the Court and Government, and of Parliament. Some three thousand people worked there.[12] Many of them were serious public servants, from the members of the Privy Council down to the humble clerks. Some were no doubt there because they sought the reflected glory and putative benefits of close proximity to the Court rather than the obscurity of living on their distant estates.

At the centre of Westminster was the vast and sprawling Whitehall Palace, built by Henry VIII around the site of Cardinal Wolsey's former residence, York Place, and now Queen Elizabeth's favourite London residence. The main section of the Palace, comprising the Royal Court, the Privy Gallery, Princes Lodgings, Council Chamber and the Palace kitchens, was grouped round the Privy garden. Numerous other buildings, including the cockpit, bowling alley and tennis courts were spread around this central group. The whole Palace covered 23 acres between the river and St James's Park, with King's Street (the present Whitehall), nominally a public highway, running through the middle. Some security was provided by the Holbein Gate and the King Street Gate at the north and south ends respectively on the central part of the highway and the Court Gate giving access to the main section of the Palace. At the southern end was the old Westminster Palace which had been badly damaged by fire early in Henry VIII's reign and was now the home of the Law Courts located in Westminster Hall, and of both Houses of Parliament, the Lords: with about ninety members, including 26 bishops, in the Parliament Chamber; and the Commons, with 460 members, in St Stephen's Chapel. Beyond was Westminster Abbey, directly facing the Archbishop of Canterbury's residence, Lambeth Palace, across the river on the south bank.[13]

Life in the City was full of contrasts.[14] Many of the streets leading down to the river were mean, crowded, noisy and smelly. Timber-framed houses were several storeys high and the gap between them across the street was narrow. The surface of the streets was made of caked mud which might, or might not, be covered with gravel or sand. Either way pedestrians, who were in the majority, had a dirty walk and those who could afford it rode on horseback. This may have raised them above the mud, but they still had to face the hazards of carts laden with commodities of all kinds and, by the end of the century, some carriages, pulled by two or four horses with a carter or coachman who gave way to no-one, and of flocks of sheep or geese being driven on their way to market. There was no such thing as a Highway Code so traffic blocks must often have rivalled even those of today, with no help from police to clear them. The stench from discarded refuse often left to rot, despite the efforts of the authorities to forbid it, from sewage, though it was usually disposed of down a shute at the side of the house into a cesspit below, and from people's bodies at a time when bathing was a rare occurrence if not an aberration, prevailed everywhere. In the meaner streets the servants' habit of emptying chamber pots out of upper storey windows, preceded by the cry of 'gardy-loo' (gardez l'eau) made the centre of the street the safest place to walk or ride.[15] Besides the hubbub generated by the throngs of people and animals the noise from the City's industries, brass-makers, pewterers, cutlers and so on, and from the constant new building during the second half of the century, must have been deafening.

There was another side to the City. The rich merchants and their wives demanded expensive high quality products and many of them indeed made their fortune through trading in such products. The grandest street was Cheapside, a wide thoroughfare with paved surface running through the heart of the City from east to west. It was lined with handsome houses and smart shops, mercers, grocers, apothecaries and so on. Towards the eastern end was Goldsmiths' Row where was to be found 'the most beautiful frame of fair houses and shops that be within the walls of London or elsewhere in England.'[16] In Cheapside and its eastern extension, Cornhill, were markets for poultry and dairy products and stalls occupied by flower and vegetable sellers. At the junction between them, the stocksmarket, were fishmongers and butchers. Markets for other products had their recognised locations in the City, under strict control of the Merchant Companies. The smarter streets in the City lay to the north of Cheapside. This was the area in which many of the leading merchants and lawyers, who constituted the elite of the City, lived. Houses were three or four storeys high with tall chimneys and windows of transparent glass. They were often jettied at first-floor level and above, which had the effect of narrowing the streets. The streets were more likely to be paved and kept cleaner and safer because the richer wards could afford to employ more scavengers and constables. But even here there was little chance of eliminating the pervasive dirt and smell which were characteristic of Tudor London. Despite the densely built streets a surprising number of houses had their own small gardens and there were spacious grounds attached to the four Inns of Court, all situated just outside the wall, and to the halls of some of the Livery Companies. The latter were all within the wall, though not all the 60 companies recorded by Stow had a hall of their own.[17]

Housewives of all social classes shopped on foot, as all lived within easy reach of the markets. Around these the chatter of the shoppers and the cries of the market stallholders and of the street vendors added to the general hubbub. The merchants' wives, smartly dressed with elaborate ruffs, befurred and bejewelled gowns and wide skirts took their maids with them to carry their purchases. The lower ranks, more simply dressed with small ruffs and slimmer skirts, carried their own. Most men could walk, if they wished, to their place of work; many lived over the shop. They showed off their legs (shapely or not) in tightly fitting breeches, with several layers of clothing above, topped by the inevitable ruff, and either a gown or a cloak thrown casually over one shoulder for outer wear. The richer the wearer, the more elaborate and highly coloured were the decorations and trimmings. Young men who fancied their appearance often wore short swords or rapiers. Working men's jerkins were of leather and their breeches of tough cheap material. They too wore ruffs, smaller in size and all men, rich and poor alike, wore tall hats or flat caps made of felt or cloth.

An easily recognised group on the streets was the apprentices in their distinctive blue outer garments, gowns in winter and calf-length coats in summer, and flat cloth caps. This was an increasingly popular form of education for country boys, often sons of yeomen or husbandmen, analogous to the legal training at the Inns of Court and Chancery for sons of the gentry. Their number trebled in the second half of the century to around five thousand.[18] There was a fair number of dropouts each year (one suspects due either to homesickness or indiscipline) and of those who stayed the course not all remained in London to pursue the trades they had learned. They were a boisterous crowd of (mostly) teenagers who behaved very much as teenagers en masse always have done without much regard to the punishment they risked having to undergo from their masters. At a lower level were the servants who, besides accompanying their mistresses to the market, were also employed in running errands and in carrying water required for domestic use, which was drawn in large conical shaped containers from the free public conduits dotted about the City supplied by pipes from springs and wells outside the wall and from the City's own rivers.

Lastly the poor, many of them beggars, were everywhere to be found. As already noted, their numbers were growing and the problem was exacerbated following the dissolution of the monasteries and other religious houses, which had done much to alleviate their distress. The removal of this tradititional call on the charity of Londoners, however, made it both necessary and possible to lay this charge both on the charity of rich citizens and on the parishes. According to the 'Custom of the City', Freemen of the City were expected to leave one third of their estates to charitable causes.[19] This custom was strictly observed by Alice and her three husbands, all of whom provided generously in their Wills for the poor of parishes with which they were associated and for the inmates of London's prisons. The poor, the sick and fatherless children were looked after in various institutions founded on the sites of former religious houses given to the City after the dissolution. Principal among these were: St Bartholomew's, long established as a hospital outside the wall to the north; Bethlehem (Bedlam) for the insane; St Thomas's, in Southwark for the aged and infirm; and Christ's Hospital (known as the 'Bluecoat School') on the site of the Greyfriars monastery, founded in 1553 as a refuge and school for orphans, of which Alice's second husband was a generous benefactor.[20] The problem of poverty, which was so evident on the City streets, was addressed in a series of measures during Elizabeth's reign, culminating in the Poor Law of 1601.[21] The second half of the 16th century was a period when the City authorities and the richer citizens took seriously their obligations towards their less fortunate fellow countrymen. Their efforts and those of the Government had the effect of mitigating the hardship though by no means of eliminating it and the resultant crime.[22]

Major crimes, such as murder and treason, as well as felonies both great and small, including rape, sodomy, embezzlement, witchcraft, robbery and many others, were all punishable by death. This was normally carried out by hanging on the gallows at Tyburn (Hyde Park Corner), but convicted heretics were burned at the stake at Smithfield, and 'if a woman poison her husband she is burned alive.'[23] Prior to her excommunication by the Pope in 1570, the Queen adopted a lenient attitude towards Catholic recusancy, involving non-attendance at church. Although strictly defined as heresy, it was normally punished by fines and only in extreme cases of persistent offence was the death penalty incurred. After 1570, however, recusancy became high treason for which the ultimate and repulsive penalty was to be hung, drawn and quartered. Many Catholic martyrs suffered in this way, and in all three hundred Catholics died for their faith in Elizabeth's reign.[24] People became inured to the gruesome public spectacles which had a macabre attraction for the crowds who gathered to watch them.

Imprisonment was not often used for criminal offences, for which besides the death sentence there was a variety of punishments. Prostitutes were dragged across the Thames behind a boat and perjurers had the letter 'P' branded on their foreheads; a spell in the stocks or pillory set up in various places in the City, including the eastern end of Cheapside, was an uncomfortable penalty for many misdemeanours. London boasted 18 prisons, including Bridewell (Henry VIII's former palace on the riverside at the western limit of the City) and the Tower, Marshalsea (in Southwark) for religious offenders and the Fleet for debtors. The conditions in them were not pleasant (except for the rich who could afford to pay for luxuries), hence the importance of private charitable bequests.

A striking feature of the City in the 16th century was the large number of churches in close proximity to one another. At the heart of the City was the vast Norman edifice of St Paul's Cathedral, which lost its spire in a lightning strike in 1561 (and was to be destroyed by fire a hundred years later). This was frequented not only by the devout who attended the services but also by a motley crowd of beggars and petty thieves who hung about the west end jostling and preying on the churchgoers. Outside in the churchyard stood the famous Paul's Cross, the venue for a weekly sermon by a succession of distinguished preachers who used the occasion to discourse on political as well as religious topics of the day. On a fine day this event attracted a congregation of several thousand (to many of whom the sermon must have been inaudible) who came not only to hear the speaker but to exchange gossip, transact business and observe the latest fashions of the rich. One cannot doubt that Alice was a frequent participant at these weekly events, whether accompanied by her husband or not. Over a hundred more churches lay within the City's boundaries. A contemporary map gives the impression that there was a church in almost every street. While this is an exaggeration, the fact is that most of them were little more than a hundred yards from their neighbours and many had only a few hundred parishioners, some even less.[25] The two churchwardens, elected annually, were responsible (as they are today) for the finances and fabric of their churches. They also administered charitable bequests for relief of the poor of the parish and were empowered to demand contributions from parishioners, in which they had the assistance of an 'Overseer'. Churchgoing on Sunday was compulsory, under threat of fine for absence, so the churches were generally packed for the morning service (Matins, not Holy Communion, for which attendance once a year at Easter was the only requirement) and congregations contained a complete mix of people of all classes, forced to endure a sermon which could last for an hour.

Though the churches were stripped of their ornate decorations and images and the religious festivals more muted than before the Reformation, the City was not lacking in colourful spectacles. The Lord Mayor's procession, which took place after his election in October, was an occasion of great pomp and pageantry. The Mayor and all the Aldermen in their scarlet liveries proceeded down the river in their highly decorated barges to Westminster, where the Mayor swore allegiance to the Queen, and returned on foot along the Strand and Fleet Street, led by the Swordbearer and other officers of the City all wearing the Mayoral livery. In August the Lord Mayor and Aldermen processed to Finsbury Fields for the opening of St Bartholomew's Fair. There were many other occasions when the Mayor wearing his livery and gold chain of office and preceded by his Swordbearer was seen about the streets of the City. The splendour of the Queen's periodic visits to the City surpassed these spectacles. She was accompanied by a vast retinue of courtiers and dignitaries, all sumptuously apparelled, to the evident delight of cheering crowds who lined the decorated streets.

So there was always plenty to watch even for those who could not afford to pay for their entertainment. 'Real' tennis and bowling were fashionable sports for the rich. Theatre-going was growing in popularity, despite the disapproval of the City's strictly Protestant governors. The latter were, however, unable to suppress it since the companies of actors had the support of the Queen and Court. By the end of the century three theatres – The Swan, the Rose and the Globe – were established in Bankside (Southwark). One cannot imagine that Alice would have been prevented by any doubts on the part of her husbands from attending performances of the plays of Christopher Marlowe, Ben Jonson and the early works of Shakespeare, such as *The Comedy of Errors* and *Romeo and Juliet*.[26] Bankside was also the location for the bull-baiting and bear-baiting pits, both highly popular forms of entertainment amongst all classes, and, notoriously, the principal location of London's 'stews' (brothels).

Many well-to-do families enjoyed musical evenings in their own homes. Most educated men played the lute and sang or accompanied the singing of songs like the perennial favourite 'Greensleeves' or madrigals such as those of Thomas Morley ('My bonny lass she smileth' and 'Now is the month of maying') and William Byrd ('This sweet and merry month of May').

This was the City in which Alice lived and brought up her children. It was noisy, dirty and smelly, but there was much to amuse and entertain its inhabitants. Alice certainly had the means and no doubt also the inclination to take full advantage of the pleasures which were available to her.

Chapter 5

Mr and Mrs Henry Robinson

Alice was married to Henry Robinson in 1570 at the age of twenty-three. No record of his date of birth has been found. But assuming that he was 16 when he started his apprenticeship as a brewer – though he could have been a little older – this would put the year of his birth as 1544, that is to say three years older than Alice.

What is certain is that Henry came from Egremont in Cumberland. The town of Egremont was founded early in Norman times, when it was intended to be the capital of the new county of Copeland. The Normans had ambitious plans to make the town a major administrative and military centre on the way to the north of England. But these plans failed and, towards the end of the 13th century, Copeland was absorbed into the existing county of Cumberland. Three hundred years later Cumberland and its neighbouring counties towards the Scottish border were, in the words of the Elizabethan topographer, William Camden, described as 'barren places which cannot easily by the painful labour of the husbandman be brought to fruitfulness'. The county had a history of violence, having been fought over by the marauding border clans, as well as by the invading Scots.

In the 14th century, Egremont itself was devastated and plundered by the Scots under Robert the Bruce, with enormous loss of life. The Norman castle remained empty for a long period after the Scots withdrew. It fell into a state of disrepair and became derelict. But at least by the middle of the 15th century, raids by the Scots into Cumberland were less frequent and Egremont was able to settle down to a relatively peaceful existence. Being remote from London, which was 275 miles away, a journey which might take up to a week on horseback depending on the weather and state of the roads, it was more directly affected by the power exercised by the major landowners than by the authority of the central government. At the start of Queen Elizabeth's reign it was a very small town of some 140 families, suggesting a total population of between 700 and 800 people. In size it was more like a large village, and the status of 'Borough' seemed hardly to suit it; in fact, as early as the end of the 13th century the burgesses had petitioned the Crown to be spared the expense of having to send two representatives to Parliament as their status required. The principal occupation of the people of Egremont was agriculture and the crafts and industries associated with it, such as corn-grinding, wool-processing for the manufacture of cloth and the tanning of skins to produce leather. Open cast mining produced a small quantity of iron ore, but the mining industry was not fully developed until two hundred years later.

By the start of the 16th century, the greater part of the Borough and Lordship of Egremont was held by the Percy family, whose vast estates extended northwards as far as the Scottish border. The small remaining part was acquired by purchase from its hereditary owners towards the end of the century. So most of the householders of Egremont were tenants of the Percys, though there were brief periods when the estates were forfeit to the Crown following the incompetence or attainder of the Earl of Northumberland. One such period was 1537-49 when the brother, and heir, of the 6th Earl (Henry Percy, Anne Boleyn's lover, who died in 1537) was under sentence of attainder for his participation in the ill-fated northern uprising against the breach with Rome known as the 'Pilgrimage of Grace'. This coincided with Henry Robinson's childhood, but would have had no practical effect on the position of the tenants.

Cumberland was a county of farmers, ignored and even derided by the people of the more prosperous south, as Camden's comment implies. The gentry owned their own estates, though those who had aspirations to be seen and heard around the Court would not spend more time on them than was necessary. They employed a manager to farm them or let part of them to tenants. The yeomen were more industrious, permanently resident and were personally involved in the work of farming their own land, whether as freeholders or fixed term leaseholders. The most successful and prosperous of them farmed land of up to about 400 acres and achieved a standard of living fully comparable with that of the gentry, into whose society in the county they were increasingly accepted (though neither would match the standard of their peers in the lusher southern counties). The lower ranks of yeoman might farm no more than 100 acres, which, however, provided sufficient produce to enable them to live in tolerable comfort. Below the yeomen in status came the husbandmen, smallholders holding properties ranging from 10 acres up to about sixty. On this they would graze sheep, pigs and horses and grow as much corn as there was space for. This was the most numerous class of small farmers, whose status roughly equated to that of skilled craftsmen. Their life was one of unremitting labour to provide a decent living to support their families. The fortunate ones would hold secure tenancies with a fixed period, but many were tenants-at-will, subject, in theory at least, to the landlord's pleasure. The husbandman was a respected figure in the community who would often, in small towns and villages, be called upon to undertake such civic duties as churchwarden or constable. Lower in the social scale came the mass of labourers who worked on the farms, the semi-skilled such as cowherds or ploughmen in reasonably secure employment but many without skills earning a precarious living with uncertain prospects.

The social distinctions represented by these levels of land ownership and management were important and generally observed strictly. But they were by no means inflexible, any more than were the corresponding categories of gentleman, merchant and craftsman. Wealth was a key factor, as in the case of the prosperous yeoman, and so were patronage and ability. There are plenty of examples of movement from one class to another in the 16th century, at all levels of society, as will be seen in the lives and fortunes of Alice and her husbands.

This then was the background for Henry's birth and childhood: a remote and entirely rural county where the principal occupation was agriculture and a small town whose population was made up of small-holding tenant farmers, like Henry's father, tradesmen supplying their wants and landless labourers, skilled and unskilled. All that is known of William Robinson is that he was a husbandman. There is nothing to show how prosperous or how prominent he was in the Egremont community. But the name Robinson recurs frequently in the records of tenants of the Borough of Egremont in the second half of the 16th century. Some certainly and no doubt most of them were related to William, whose known family is described below. Robinson was one of the commonest surnames in Cumberland and Westmorland as well as in the other counties of the north of England.[1] Given the lack of documentary records, it is difficult to establish how far the different families were connected. But there is at least some circumstantial evidence pointing to links between the Egremont Robinsons and Robinson families in Westmorland and Yorkshire.[2]

William Robinson had three sons and one daughter. Given the gaps in ages between the sons it is quite likely that he had other children, who may have died unrecorded, in childbirth or infancy. Nothing is known of his wife or whether he was married more than once. The eldest son, William, was apprenticed to the Brewers' Company in London in 1539 which would put the year of his birth as about 1524. There are also good grounds for assuming that the second son, Richard, became an apprentice brewer in 1547, which would mean he was born about 1532.[3] So William and Richard would have been 19 and 11 years older respectively than their youngest brother, Henry. The daughter, Elizabeth, married Richard Hazy of Clifton, in Cumberland. Her place in the family is not known, but since she was a widow by the time Henry died she was probably not the younger of the four children. No children of Elizabeth are mentioned.

William, the eldest brother, did not become a Freeman of the Brewers' Company after completing his apprenticeship; he returned to Egremont, where he is shown as a tenant of the Borough in 1578 and of other land nearby amounting to about 60 acres, with barns and other buildings. He almost certainly died before 1585 since he is the only one of the family not mentioned in Henry's Will. Richard also did not continue his profession as a brewer but returned to Egremont after his apprenticeship, where he married and had a son, Richard, a daughter, Jane, and other children. In 1578 both Richard and the son are shown as tenants of the Borough and of farms in the demesne land of the Egremont Lordship. By that time Richard was evidently a man of substance in the Egremont community and was recognised as such in Henry's Will.

But it is with Henry, as Alice's future husband, that this story is principally concerned. Henry began his career as a brewer when he started his apprenticeship in the Brewers' Company in August 1559, thus following in the footsteps of his elder brothers. It must have been a somewhat alarming experience for a boy of 15, coming from rural Cumberland, to be plunged into the totally different world of the City of London, nearly 300 miles away from home. Moreoover, he was by then fatherless, though the year of his father's death is not known. It was, no doubt, of some comfort – to his mother as well as to Henry – that a place was secured for him with the same family as had cared for his brother, Richard, 12 years earlier.

Cumberland's farmers provided a major source of apprentices to the Brewers' Company in the years between 1540 and 1600. Of a total of 140 London brewers' apprentices who came from the county during this period, 105 were sons of husbandmen and 11 sons of yeomen, leaving only 24 from families having other craft backgrounds. Seven of the 140 came from Egremont, all but one being sons of husbandmen. Unlike Henry many of the other boys, his brothers included, did not remain in the brewing trade in London after completing their apprenticeships. But those who returned to Cumberland, or moved elsewhere, would have acquired a better education and a more thorough grounding in a skilled craft than they would have done had they remained at home.

The master to whom Richard and Henry were apprenticed became a great figure in the Brewers' Company. William Beswicke took his first four apprentices in the 1540s. During the next four decades he took on a further 31, the last in 1583. A further nine started with him and were passed on to other masters, presumably because he had already reached his quota in those years. Beswicke was elected the first single Master of the Brewers' Company in 1563; he was re-elected in 1564, an unusual honour. Even then his colleagues on the Court would not let him go! He was brought back as Master in 1577 and re-elected in 1578, the only Master until the First World War to achieve the double twice! Henry Robinson was fortunate to be introduced to the 'mistery' of brewing by such a highly experienced apprentice master.

For the next seven or eight years Henry was hard at work (it must be assumed) following the strict regime for an apprentice in the Brewers' Company. Though he maintained a close connection with his family and an affection for Egremont for the rest of his life, he can only seldom, if at all, have been able to return during this period. He was half way through his apprenticeship when William Beswicke served his first two years as Master of the Company. No doubt this will have given him some insight into the way in which the Company was run, which will have stood him in good stead when he became one of the Wardens in 1580. But Mrs Beswicke, who knew the family, having had his elder brother Richard in her care, must have been a major influence in his life during his adolescence. At any rate he was the only one of the three Robinson brothers who decided to pursue a career in brewing. He became a Freeman of the company in 1569.

By this time Henry had set up in business as a brewer and took on his first apprentice. He was shortly to take on further apprentices for whom he would need to provide not only the training but also the home life which he had enjoyed. In short, he needed a wife and, in the following year, he found one. His marriage to Alice was a major event which was to last for the rest of his life. So it is time to take up her story, which will mean going back some years. What had happened to Alice since her father's death in 1558 and how did she meet Henry Robinson?

It has been suggested that Alice spent much time with her recently married sister, Margery Draper. There is certainly no evidence to suppose that she had much to do with her guardian, Robert Wood, and her stepmother, newly widowed and with three young children to look after, would have been glad to have Alice taken off her hands. No doubt Alice too, already, at 12, legally of age, was happy to leave the more restricted home to which her younger half-siblings and their mother moved on leaving the spacious quarters of her father's inn. So Alice may well have gone to live with the Drapers from the early 1560s onwards, taking with her the young girl who had witnessed the incident of the arrow. Margery and her husband had a house in Islington, in St John's Street, and another in Stroud Green, as well as property in the City of London. Their eldest son, Thomas, was born in Islington and baptised at St Mary's Church, and of course Alice's brother Robert continued to live in the parish. So Alice had ample opportunity for maintaining her family connections there.

Alice's elementary education in Islington has already been described in Chapter 2; by the time she joined her sister it can be taken for granted that she was able to read (though not to write which she probably never learned) and had learned some of the household skills every woman needed. And, as a matter of course, she would already be used to riding on horseback. At the Drapers' house she would learn more, alongside an elder sister who was herself newly married, about cooking, sewing, spinning and weaving and how to manage a household. These subjects formed the basis of every young girl's education. But by the middle of the century, opportunities for much wider education were becoming accessible to girls of merchant and other middle-class families, whereas they had hitherto been confined to the aristocracy and gentry. So it is quite probable that Alice had lessons in French, science, history and music. By the mid-1560s Margery must have been on the look-out for a suitable husband for her sister, someone of similar social background and religion and within a few years of her age. What more natural than that she should turn her attention to a young man known to – and perhaps recommended by – one of her husband's fellow brewers. William Beswicke's wife may have had similar thoughts about securing a wife for Henry Robinson, perhaps one of the favourites among her husband's former apprentices. So it is not wholly fanciful to suggest that this was how Alice and Henry were brought together.

Alice and Henry's betrothal took place in the summer of 1570. This involved a firm commitment on their parts to get married later in the year. Once betrothed Alice would wear a gold ring on the fourth finger of her right hand. They were to be married at St Dunstan-in-the-West, a 13th-century church on the north side of Fleet Street between Chancery Lane and Fetter Lane.[4] This was the parish church of the Draper family, though they also had connections with St Bride's, Fleet Street. John Draper was a major owner of property in the City, as well as in Essex and Middlesex. His principal residence was in the Blackfriars, just on the south side of Fleet Street and Ludgate Hill, and his main brewhouse was situated in the Whitefriars district between Fleet Street and the River Thames. St Dunstan's was also the parish church of Henry Robinson, who made his home with Alice in Chancery Lane, where he was living at the time of his marriage.[5]

What Alice brought with her by way of a dowry is not known. No provision was made for this in her father's Will, 12 years earlier. Would Robert Wood, her formal guardian, have seen this as part of the duty laid on him by his friend, Thomas Wilkes? Otherwise the provision would have been left to the generosity of Alice's brother, already in business but as yet unmarried, and her sister. It is just possible (though unlikely) that Henry's own prospects – and Alice's personal attractions – were together sufficiently alluring that he was willing to take her without a dowry! At any rate the banns were called on three successive Sundays at St Dunstan's and, no impediment having been raised, Alice and Henry were married on 26 August 1570. Alice wore a white gown with a small cap and gloves. The wedding ceremony took place in the church porch, where the ring was transferred to the bride's left hand by the bridegroom, using the same words as in the modern marriage service: 'With this ring I thee wed; with my body I thee worship', and the same vows: 'I, Henry, take thee, Alice, to have and to hold, for better, for worse, till death us do part.' The wedding party then moved into the body of the church for the marriage service of prayers, sermon and perhaps some singing of metric psalms (hymns were not introduced until much later) and organ playing. The service would be followed by the 'wedding breakfast', an occasion for a prolonged party which was traditionally held in the bridegroom's house, and at which no doubt much home brewed beer was drunk. If this practice was followed, the event would have taken place in Henry Robinson's house in Chancery Lane. At the end of the day it is unlikely that Alice and Henry escaped the customary ribaldry when they retired for the night. The honeymoon had not yet been invented so Henry was quickly back to work as Alice assumed her household duties.

In terms of the Common Law as it applied in the 16th century, a woman on marriage became a 'chattel' of her husband, subject to his control and guidance, and he became possessed of all her worldly goods. This certainly provided a remedy for a husband in extreme cases, though it was a long time before wives had any corresponding remedy against cruel husbands. But it is hard to imagine Alice becoming a chattel of anyone, and to judge from the circumstances of her life with Henry Robinson and from the tributes paid to her in the Wills of her two later husbands, none of them had any need or wish to enforce their legal rights!

After visiting England at the end of the century, the Duke of Wurtemburg wrote that: 'England is a paradise for women, a prison for servants and a hell for horses.'[6] This was surely an exaggeration on all three counts, but there were no doubt elements of truth in it. Horses were the principal, indeed the only, means by which most people could travel on land, unless they went on foot. Everyone who could afford one owned a horse, and those who couldn't hired them when needed. Certainly, they were pressed hard on long journeys and often belaboured to the point of cruelty, but it cannot have been in the owner's interest seriously to maltreat his own horses. But even in such circles as the royal palace of Whitehall the vicious baiting, to the point of killing, of horses, sometimes with a monkey as rider, by fierce dogs was evidently an acceptable form of entertainment. Perhaps the Duke had witnessed such events, though the English were certainly no more cruel than other Europeans. Servants, especially at the lower levels, endured a life of drudgery, under strict discipline with severe penalties for disobedience or misdemeanours and under constant fear of dismissal. But at least they were provided with bed, food and clothes, and were in this respect better off than the vast hordes of landless unemployed, even those lucky enough to receive parish poor relief. No doubt many servants were harshly treated, but not all mistresses were inhumane. Alice's known character does not suggest that her 'prison' regime was unduly callous by 16th-century standards.

If one can ignore their legal position, in practice the freedom enjoyed by women in England was much greater than that of their counterparts in continental Europe. To this extent the Duke's observation was justified, in so far as concerned the wives of the gentry and well-to-do merchants. Alice was free to do her own shopping in the market, at Newgate, Billingsgate or Leadenhall, and to visit the mercers' and goldsmiths' shops which were to be found in the City, especially in the fashionable area of Cheapside where Henry's cousin, John Robinson, Freeman of the Mercers' Company, had his establishment. She could also enjoy an active social life with her women friends, with whom she might play cards, make music and perhaps also dance.

But how much time did she have for such leisure pursuits? Her first duty was to run the household. This meant not only managing the servants, of whom the Robinsons may have had up to half a dozen in their early days and a larger number as the family increased in prosperity and size. She would also be involved in carrying out some of the tasks herself. This was a responsible and very demanding role which every housewife had to play. Her servants, being mostly young and inexperienced, would require initiation in the preparation of different types of food: baking bread, curing hams, salting meat, making jellies and preserves, and so on, as well as in the way to serve meals. She would have to ensure that the rushes covering the floors, which easily became unhygienic and harboured disease, were renewed regularly. Alice would also have to be ready to deal with sickness or injury to members of her household, which would involve knowledge of the medicinal properties of herbs and plants. Laundry was a hard task involving the soaping, rinsing, beating – with wooden bats, smoothing, with an iron heated on the fire, and folding of heavy linen sheets and articles of clothing. Alice may have been able to arrange for the sheets, in particular, to be taken away and done by a laundress who would spread them out to dry on the fields and open spaces at the outskirts of the City.

This is not an exhaustive list. One might conclude that it is little more than the role of a modern mother with a house and family to run. But that would be to overlook the total lack of equipment, mechanical or otherwise, the minimal education of most servants and the absence of expert knowledge and sources of advice built up and developed over several hundred years which are available today. In addition it would be Alice's job to look after the garden, which was a feature of many houses in the City of London, much more than is the case today. William Harrison's London garden in 1579 was only 300 feet square but he grew 300 medicinal herbs in it.

Finally, but in fact first in priority as being the primary purpose of marriage, was the bearing of children. Women in the early years of their marriage were expected to be almost perpetually pregnant. 'Great bellied' was a term of approbation, with no hint of vulgarity about it. Alice certainly did her duty in this department. But childbirth was a hazardous occupation as she was soon to discover.

All in all, the burdens borne by a housewife were heavy, in extent and responsibility. The Duke of Wurtemburg's 'paradise' was no doubt an apt description when applied to women at the highest levels of society, in terms of wealth and status. But for most wives it was a relative term, or a state to be achieved late in life after child-bearing and with a husband who had made his pile in the City. The Duke may have experienced what Erasmus in the early years of the 16th century had found so delightful about English women: 'Wherever you go, everyone welcomes you with a kiss and the same on bidding farewell. If you were once to taste them, and find how delicate and fragrant they are, you would certainly desire till death to be a sojourner in England.'[7] Perhaps the Duke meant to say – or should have added – 'paradise for men'!

Alice's first child, John, was born in 1572. Being her first, she may well have breast-fed him herself, though it is likely that she employed a wet-nurse for her subsequent children. Childbirth which normally took place in the mother's house was a painful and dangerous experience, with no modern methods of alleviating the suffering. Within a month or so of her delivery Alice would have undergone the ceremony of 'churching' at St Dunstan's, which combined the ancient Judaic rite of 'cleansing' with the more appropriate purpose of thanksgiving for the birth of the child and for having survived the ordeal. Traditionally, until she had been 'churched' Alice would not have re-emerged in social life. (This somewhat archaic ceremony survived in some parts of the Church of England until the middle of the 20th century.)

This was the start of a constant series of pregnancies for Alice, though sadly few of the children survived infancy or childhood. John was only three when he died; the second and third children, Henry (born in 1573) and William (1575), both died before they were ten. Then, in 1576, Alice had a daughter, Margaret, who survived and whose story is told in Chapter 6. She was followed by three more children, Ann (1577), Susan (1578) and Thomas (1579), all of whom died in infancy. Thereafter she had better luck with two girls, Alice (1581) and Anne (1582), who both lived to marry and have children of their own. Then at last she managed to produce two sons who survived, though the first, John, born in 1583, only lived until the age of fourteen. Her youngest son, Henry, born in February 1586 after his father's death, lived to be the inheritor of the Cransley estate and founder of the family of Robinson of Cransley (see Chapters 7 and 12).

Though Alice was so frequently 'great-bellied' she had no need for special maternity clothes. Women's dress was sufficiently loose-fitting and adaptable to allow for comfort at a time when their lot was to endure constant pregnancies. In bed she wore a loose fitting smock, which in the morning was replaced by a 'nightgown' with long sleeves and a soft collar, made of satin or taffeta, for her daily business about the house. As her husband became more prosperous, for social occasions and for shopping in the fashionable districts of the City, her clothes were more elaborate. The basic garment was a full length chemise with a petticoat over it. Then came a bodice, in two parts laced at the sides and with detachable sleeves, and a separate skirt. On top of all this was a loose gown, fitted across the shoulders and falling in set folds spreading outwards to the ground, probably made of silk and lined with velvet. At times when she had a figure to show off – which were rare during her marriage to Henry – she may have worn a full-length gown fitted at the waist and extended from the hips to fall loosely over the skirt, which possibly had the stiff hoops of a Spanish farthingale to support it underneath.[8] Gaps in the outer garments were deliberately placed to expose the decoration of those beneath, all in single colours, gold, red, yellow and black being the ones principally used. As she grew older, she replaced the soft collar with a ruff, as shown in her picture, with its multitude of pleats held in place by wire and requiring to be regularly washed and starched. The high-crowned hat, which she had worn in Islington (and which had been pierced by the famous arrow), the normal style for a countrywoman, was replaced by a smaller conical type of hood or cap, made of velvet or ermine and worn on the back of the head, with jewels on the rounded front border. On her feet she wore low-cut slippers of cloth or thin leather and she put on overshoes to cover her feet and ankles when going out into the ever dirty streets. And of course, indispensable for any housewife, was the belt with such essential accessories as scissors, fan, pomander ball, mirror, all attached to it by ribbon.

What of the children? Alice's daughters, once they got out of their simple baby clothes, aged about four, wore long frocks with aprons over them until they were six or seven. Only Margaret, Alice and Anne were to live beyond this age, at which they adopted dress which was, in miniature, similar in style to that of an adult. Boys followed much the same process; they were 'breeched' at the age of seven, an important step when they discarded the childish gown and put on adult male clothes. John, for a short time only, and Henry would both reach this stage, but not until the 1590s long after their father's death.

While Alice was engaged in having children and running the household, Henry was at work at his brewhouse. This was in Blackfriars, but he may also have brewed beer at the house in Chancery Lane. His business clearly prospered and he was able to extend the Blackfriars property in 1578. By this time 'hopping beer' was well established and had replaced the traditional English ale as the favoured drink. Compare this praise for hops, written in 1576, with the derogatory attitude expressed by Andrew Borde over thirty years earlier (see Chapter 3):

> In favour of the hoppe thus much I say, that whereas you cannot make above 8 or 9 gallons of indifferent ale out of one bushell of malt, you may draw 18 or 20 gallons of very good beer, neither is the hoppe more profitable to enlarge the quantity of your drinke than necessary to prolong the continuance thereof. For if your ale may endure a fortnight, your Beere through the benefit of the Hoppe shall continue a month and what grace yieldeth to the taste, all men may judge that have sense in their mouths here in our country ale giveth place unto Beere, and most of our countrymen do abhore and abandon ale as a loathsome drink.[9]

No reference now to the hops' tendency to 'inflate the bely'!

Work started early at the brewery. The apprentices, as described in Chapter 3, were expected to work hard and their day started before 6a.m. By 1570 Henry had taken on three, and three more joined him in the next five years, one being Thomas Robinson, the son of his brother Richard. He seems to have taken 10 years to complete his apprenticeship, perhaps because he enjoyed his aunt's hospitality! A further eight were spread over the next 10 years, of whom three had not finished their term before Henry died and were transferred to other masters. Looking after the welfare of the apprentices was one of Alice's responsibilities; she would see that they were provided with breakfast of small beer and bread before they started work in the morning and that a cooked dinner was provided around midday, meat on most days but fish on Friday, with by this time some green vegetables which were beginning to enter the popular diet. After work there would be supper about six in the evening and early bed to avoid, as far as possible, the expensive use of candles.

The Robinsons and Drapers were near neighbours, so the two sisters were able to keep in close touch. Both families attended St Dunstan's church and no doubt the cousins were friends, though there was a big gap in ages. Margery's eldest son, Thomas, was eight years older than Alice's first-born son, and Anne, Margery's elder daughter, was born a year or two earlier. By the time Margaret, Alice's first daughter to survive childhood, was born, John Draper had died. Margery continued to run her husband's brewing business after his death and took on an apprentice in 1580. But she was probably relieved to hand over the management to her sons Thomas and Henry when they came of age. They are recorded as taking on their first apprentices in

1585 and 1587 respectively. Sometime later Margery moved to the house in Stroud Green (Islington) which was her home until she died. (One of John Draper's more interesting bequests was 'ten pounds of money towards the amendment of the highway between King's Cross and my house in Stroud Green'.) As a widow Margery was a rich woman, with rents from properties in London and neighbouring counties left to her by her husband.

Anne, who was no more than 15 when her father died, was the first of the Draper children to be married. Alice, who was her godmother, always took a special interest in her; she was the only one of her nephews and nieces whom Alice mentioned in her Will. Her husband, Eustace Bedingfield, came from the Bedingfield family of Oxburgh Hall in Norfolk, which had twice been cast in difficult roles earlier in the century. Eustace's grandfather, Sir Edmund Bedingfield, was given custody of Queen Catherine at Kimbolton Castle after she had been divorced by Henry VIII. He was to report to Thomas Cromwell on the serious decline in her health which led to her death, exacerbated by pressures brought on her to swear the Oath of Supremacy, and was in charge of her funeral procession to Peterborough Cathedral. His eldest son, Sir Henry Bedingfield, Eustace's uncle, was Governor of the Tower when Princess Elizabeth was committed there by her sister Mary on suspicion of complicity in Wyatt's rebellion and accompanied her when she was transferred to the Manor of Woodstock. He is said to have been a conscientious but reluctant jailor whose relations with the future Queen remained formally correct despite the aggravation her provocative behaviour caused him. Elizabeth evidently bore him no personal ill-will, though she did not, as sometimes claimed, visit him at Oxburgh during her Royal Progress to Norwich in 1578.[10]

Whatever the Queen's personal feelings may have been such a visit would not have been possible. Henry Bedingfield who, like his father, was a staunch Catholic, did not escape being penalised by the Council for recusancy and refusal to conform. Along with the leading Catholics he had been removed from the Council on the Queen's accession. But it must be assumed that Eustace, in common with many of his contemporaries, had adapted to the realities of the Elizabethan Settlement. Otherwise he would hardly have been accepted as a suitable match for one of the Protestant Draper family. Not only was he accepted but he was clearly liked and respected by his wife's two uncles, Robert Wilkes and Henry Robinson, since both of them were to make him a supervisor of their Wills.

Then suddenly in 1585 Henry Robinson fell ill. He made his Will on 15 August, 'sick in body yet in good and perfect remembrance'. He died a week later at the age of 42 and was buried at St Dunstan's. He left a son and three daughters and his widow three months' pregnant with the child who was to become his son and heir. Neither Alice nor Margery attended the funeral; this was strictly a men-only event. The principal mourners were Henry's brother-in-law, Robert Wilkes, Eustace Bedingfield and Thomas Draper, his nephew, who was, with Eustace, co-supervisor of his Will. Other male members of the family, fellow Freemen of the Brewers' Company and friends, plus people who just wanted to be seen to be present, would also be there. Funerals were major religious and social events; the funeral cortège, all wearing black, would process from the house to the church and the service would be followed by an elaborate feast, provided by Alice, though it is unlikely that she herself took part, for at least the family and close friends, and as many hangers-on as could succeed in getting admitted. The wake was an occasion for mourning the departed, but soon, as the day drew on, became a celebratory party. This is not to imply that many of those present were not sad at the loss of their friend or relative; rather that, at a time when expectation of life was short and the threat of sudden death from disease or other causes was ever present, their continued survival was a cause for rejoicing and thanksgiving.

Probate was granted for Henry's Will on 7 September to Alice and her brother Robert, the joint executors. According to 'the custom of the City' Henry left one third of his estate to his wife, one third to his children and the remaining third for charitable and other bequests. The main beneficiaries of the last third were his brother, Richard, and sister, Elizabeth, in Egremont, other members of his and Alice's family and many individual friends, colleagues, servants and former apprentices. His charitable bequests included money for poor parishioners of St Dunstan's and St Brides' churches and for prisoners in the Marshalsea and other London prisons; £20 for an annual distribution 'in perpetuity' to be made by four 'substantial' residents to 30 poor people of Egremont; and 40 shillings to the Brewers' Company 'to make them a drinking withal when the Warden thinks good'. Black mourning gowns and coats, essential wear for all those having any connection with the deceased, were to be provided for several of Henry's relatives and for 20 parishioners of St Dunstan's and 20 persons nominated by the Brewers' Company.[11]

So ended Alice's life with Henry Robinson. Theirs was a not untypical Elizabethan success story. Neither of them came from the bottom of the social scale. Henry was the youngest son of a Cumbrian smallholder and Alice the younger daughter of an Islington innkeeper. He rose to become a Freeman of the Worshipful Company of Brewers and a Citizen of London. She was the widow of a rich City merchant from whom she inherited a fortune and was to continue for many years her course of upward mobility. How she spent her inheritance is recounted in Chapter 7.

a convinced Calvinist, who held government appointments under Edward VI, succeeded in remaining in office under Queen Mary and became in 1566 a distinguished Chancellor of the Exchequer to Queen Elizabeth until his death 23 years later. Mildmay, and others such as Elkin who thought like him, though not necessarily fully sharing his Calvinist convictions, were concerned about the ignorance of so many parish priests and the dearth of educated men among the new generation of clergy in the Church of England following the departure of many Roman Catholics for English seminaries established abroad at Douai, Rome and elsewhere. To meet this perceived, and urgent, need Mildmay founded Emmanuel College, Cambridge in 1583. The College was to be restricted to students of theology who would be trained as pastors 'to labour in preaching the Word' throughout the country. In granting a licence for the new college Queen Elizabeth accused him of having 'erected a Puritan foundation', a charge which he adroitly sidestepped by denying that he would ever 'countenance anything contrary to your established laws.'[17] William Elkin left money in his Will to establish two scholarships at Emmanuel College; his widow, Alice, who added to her husband's bequest, was charged with the nomination of candidates for these for the rest of her life.[18]

Alice's status was immediately enhanced by her marriage to William. Her new husband had just completed his first term as Master of the City's senior Livery Company and, in the year of his marriage, was elected Sheriff of the City and to the life office of Alderman. He could look forward to the prospect of eventual election as Lord Mayor and even to the possibility of a knighthood. As his wife, Alice attended many of the social and ceremonious functions of the City and the Company. She had become a recognised player in the society of the London merchant class. And as a dutiful wife she was soon to make her contribution. Fifteen months after her marriage she produced a daughter, Ursula. So William became a father at last, at the age of 64, an achievement of which he was no doubt justifiably proud. But for Alice, at the age of 40, the enterprise was a hazardous one in the 16th century, even though she had been through the experience 11 times before (and this was to be the last). Ursula and her mother thrived, and the baptism took place at St Lawrence, Jewry, at the south end of Basinghall Street.

The arrival of a new baby, to add to her existing Robinson family, the youngest of whom, Henry was still only 18 months old, must have imposed a heavy burden on Alice. She was of course provided with an adequate staff of servants, but, besides her tasks of running the household, she had also some official engagements to undertake with her husband, whose prominent position no doubt drew her into a more active social life. All this left her with less time than she would have wished to supervise the education of her eldest daughter, Margaret Robinson, who was coming towards the end of her childhood. So the Elkins decided to follow the course, which was customary at that period, of placing Margaret in the care of a family who would take on this responsibility. For this purpose they chose Richard Wright, a Freeman of the Ironmongers' Company, and his wife who lived in the Blackfriars district.

The Wrights clearly took their duties seriously, and not surprisingly Margaret regarded them as very strict. Her sojourn with the Wrights came to an end as a result of a distressing episode which occurred when she was twelve. There is no reason to doubt the authenticity of the extraordinary story which was related in a London newspaper over forty years ago based on detailed research of the records of the Star Chamber.[19]

The story is of Margaret's abduction by a young man, John Skinner, who had first seen her on New Year's Day 1589, fell in love with her immediately and wanted to marry her. This at least was the message relayed to Margaret by Jane Scott, described as her 'cousin' but exact relationship uncertain, accompanied by assurances that he would treat her with kindness as a husband and by gifts as tokens of his love, which she returned. Unwisely she expressed her willingness to meet the young man provided he did not attempt to visit her in the presence of Martha Wright, who would be very angry. On one Sunday at the end of January, when she became detached from the Wrights among the large congregation emerging after morning service at the Blackfriars church of St Andrew by the Wardrobe, Jane caught hold of her and insisted on speaking with her. Against her protests, Margaret was hustled away by Jane and a friend in the direction of the river. At a certain point a number of men, armed with swords, issued from a tavern and surrounded Margaret. One of them, 21-year-old John Skinner, picked her up and carried her bodily into a waiting wherry, while his friends blocked the path of several people who, realising what was happening, had set off in pursuit through the narrow street.

As the boatman rowed the couple up the Thames towards Westminster, Margaret, so the story goes, succumbed to the romantic excitement of her situation and allowed herself to be kissed; an embrace which some witnesses later claimed to have observed. (The possibility that John might have been motivated by the knowledge that she was the heiress to a considerable fortune under her father's Will is unlikely to have passed through the mind of the young girl.) They arrived at Skinner's house in Westminster, where Lord Morley, Deputy Commissioner of Essex, lodged and, evidently intrigued by Skinner's plot, had offered his help. (Margaret's armed 'escorts' were said to have been his servants.) The young couple were not long undisturbed. In the early evening William Elkin, who had traced the couple to Westminster, arrived with half a dozen men and a warrant to search the house. Margaret was quickly hidden by Lord Morley who refused to allow entry to his room. Elkin was told that the couple had left and, after searching the rest of the house, departed empty-handed.

Next day Lord Morley arranged for his personal chaplain to marry John and Margaret, who at 12, was legally of age. The Elkins brought a case against Skinner in the Court of the Star Chamber. The trial dragged on owing to disagreement between the witnesses until the end of May 1589, when John Skinner suddenly disappeared. There were rumours that he had been murdered, but his body was never discovered and no evidence was adduced. Others claimed that Elkin had contrived to have him transported out of the country to get him out of sight and out of mind. Though the mystery was never resolved, the Court apparently presumed his death and the case was allowed to lapse. Morley appears not to have suffered for his overt complicity.

After this desperate escapade, Alice and William's first priority was to find a suitable husband for Margaret. They were successful in doing this remarkably quickly. Margaret's personal attractions added to the dowry she brought with her no doubt helped. Even so she was only just 15 when she married John Brett at St Michael's, Bassishaw, in May 1591, still below the normal age for marriage of a young woman of her class. John Brett had been educated at Lincoln College, Oxford and at the time of the marriage was aged thirty-four. He was a wealthy landowner, the owner of several country estates and a house in Chancery Lane, where the couple lived.[20]

In the same year Elkin served as Master of the Mercers' Company for the second time. The annual Election Dinner took place in the previous September. This was a splendid occasion attended only by the Liverymen of the Company, all of whom were expected to be present. Alice, with their wives, also took part but the ladies were seated in a separate room. Venison was the main dish, and other varieties of meat would also be served: leg of mutton stuffed with garlic, capon boiled with leeks, shoulder of veal, turkey and wildfowl, all placed on the table at the same time. For dessert they would be offered a selection of fruits (roasted apples and pears), jellies, tarts and cakes. The chief waiters were chosen from among the yeomen of the Company. At the end of the meal came the 'garland ceremony' in which the new Master and Wardens were decorated with diadems of gillyflowers and toasted by their predecessors from cups of hippocras or spiced wine. Other dinners took place throughout the year but this was the grandest occasion in the social programme, the opportunity for the senior members to indulge in an extravagant celebration in honour of their newly appointed officers.

Not long after his period in office ended disaster struck. The London of Queen Elizabeth's reign had already suffered from several virulent epidemics of the plague, which had been endemic in the crowded streets of the city since the Black Death two centuries earlier. It recurred towards the end of 1592 and on this occasion lasted for a year. William Elkin fell victim to it and died in October 1593. He was one of 5,390 people who, according to Stow, died from this cause in the City of London, a large proportion of the total of 8,600 deaths from all diseases. Sir William Rowe, the Lord Mayor (who had been Elkin's sponsor for his Aldermanship of Cripplegate), died while in office a week before Elkin and two other Aldermen also fell victim.[21] Alice and the children survived; it may be supposed that, like many others who were able to do so, they fled from London while the epidemic was raging but that his commitments prevented William from accompanying them. William's death occurred before he had acquired sufficient seniority on the list of Aldermen for nomination as a candidate for Lord Mayor. Poor Alice! She not only lost her husband, father and stepfather of her children, but also her hopes of becoming the wife of the highest ranking and most powerful official in the City.

By his Will, William followed the custom of the City by leaving one third of his possessions to Alice and another third to his daughter, Ursula. This amounted to a considerable fortune for each, as the distribution of the third part to charitable causes and individuals clearly indicates. Among the charities which benefited, the principal ones, besides Emmanuel College already mentioned, were his birthplace in Shropshire, the Chapelry of Ore and the parish of Mucklestone; his neighbours in the parish of St Michael, Bassishaw and the poor of other London parishes with which he had connections; and the children in Christ's Hospital, Bridewell. Other legacies went to the Mercers' Company to pay for a dinner in the Mercers' Hall for the Lord Mayor, Sheriffs and Aldermen and their wives and for the furnishing of the Hall. In addition there were some fifty legacies to named individuals, many of them relatives, including a generally expressed bequest of various sums to his poor relatives in Shropshire and Staffordshire. At his request, Elkin was buried in the church of St Michael le Querne ('at the corn') in Cheapside where his brother Richard had been buried 20 years earlier. True to his Protestant convictions he ordered that there should be 'no ringing of bells at my burial; one peal to warn people to church and one for the sermon'.

For Alice one important step remained to be taken, both in her husband's memory and for the future benefit of his daughter. This was to obtain the grant of a coat of arms for William. Only by achieving this could she secure his posthumous acceptance in the rank of 'gentleman'. Whether or not he had applied for a grant in his lifetime and failed is not clear. At any rate he died without having achieved it. But Alice was not one to be deterred by this obstacle. So she vigorously pursued with the College of Arms her claim for retrospective approval of this symbol of her late husband's gentility. And against all the odds she was successful, not only in the grant to William but in gaining recognition for Ursula as the legitimate heir to her father's arms. The arms were granted by Garter King of Arms in the 36th year of the reign of Queen Elizabeth to 'William Elkin, late Citizen and Alderman of London' and, in the same grant, their use was allowed to 'Ursula, his only daughter and sole heir.' The grant was confirmed in May 1594, six months after William's death. The record of this grant is accompanied by the comment of the York Herald of Arms that: 'Never any King of Armes could make a man a gentleman after his death but this garter.'[22] At a period when so much significance was attached to social status, this could only be seen as a decided boost to Ursula's marriage prospects.

Chapter 7

Cransley

By this time Alice was the possessor of a considerable fortune. She had inherited one third, and more, of the estates of two rich merchants in the City of London. She had all the comforts of a town house in Basinghall Street with a full complement of household servants. Her eldest daughter, Margaret, now aged 17, had been married for two years and had started a family of her own. Five children were still living at home: Alice and Anne Robinson, aged 12 and 11 respectively; the two little Robinson boys, John, aged ten and Henry, seven; and her only child by William Elkin, Ursula, aged six. At the age of 46, Alice had come a long way from her childhood as the younger daughter of an Islington innkeeper. She lacked two things which would place her firmly in the class of 'landed gentry': a coat of arms and a country estate. The first would be remedied within two years. Soon after William Elkin's death she took steps to acquire an estate, though it was one on which she herself never lived.

An opportunity to achieve this arose in 1594, most probably through the good offices of Thomas Owen, an eminent lawyer who would shortly become Alice's third husband. As recorded in Chapters 6 and 9 Thomas was a neighbour in Bassishaw, a close friend of William Elkin and a fellow Mercer. He had frequent dealings with William Cecil, Lord Burghley, and his younger son, Robert, in a professional capacity and was on personal terms with both of them. So it is likely that he learned from them of Burghley's elder son, Thomas Cecil's wish to dispose of his property at Cransley, a small settlement near Kettering in Northamptonshire.

At the beginning of Queen Elizabeth's reign the Cransley property was divided between two families, the Barnwells and the Dalysons. It consisted of three Manors, the advowson of St Andrew's Church and certain messuages (farmhouses with small holdings) which were not part of the manorial estates. The total area amounted to approximately 2,000 acres.[1] In 1575 Thomas Cecil, who after a somewhat dissolute youth had just been knighted by the Queen at Kenilworth, signed a Deed with Edward Barnwell by which he exchanged the Manor of Beeston and Mileham in Norfolk for Pulton's and Newark Manors in Cransley. Ten years later, Thomas acquired the third Cransley Manor, Merston, from Edward Dalyson, together with the rest of the property in Cransley in Dalyson's possession and the advowson of the church.[2]

Thomas Cecil was almost certainly an 'absentee landlord' for most of the 20 years that he held property in Cransley, though his father and his much younger step-brother may have done their best to ensure that this rather boorish member of the family did not spend longer than was necessary at Court. It must, however, be assumed that he modernised one of the existing houses for use during his visits, infrequent though they may have been, and as a base for his spell as Member of Parliament for Northamptonshire in 1592. The only remaining evidence of Cecil's tenure of the property is a tablet showing his coat of arms, which was incorporated in the west wall of Cransley Hall when it was built nearly 100 years after he gave up the estates (see Chapter 12). The location of the Hall was then – and is still today – on the site of the former Dalyson's Manor House which was included in Thomas Cecil's 1585 purchase and is situated about 200 yards to the south-east of the Church.[3] All this seems to indicate that Cecil used Dalyson's as his Cransley residence and that Alice's heirs also lived there until it was pulled down and replaced by the late 17th-century building which was subsequently enlarged to become the present-day Hall. It suggests that Dalyson's Manor House, even as modernised by Cecil, cannot have been especially remarkable as an example of medieval or Elizabethan manorial architecture. Nor, from Cecil's point of view, had it need to be, in view of the family's residences elsewhere and his prospective inheritance of Cecil House in the Strand and Burleigh House in Lincolnshire on the death of his father and his succession to the title as the 2nd Lord Burghley, which took place in 1598.

Sir Thomas Cecil conveyed the Manors and other Cransley property to Alice in 1595. The conveyance was made to Alice in the name of Alice Elkin, widow, and so must have been completed early in the year, since she was to marry Thomas Owen on 3 March 1595. Unfortunately there is no record in the Cecil family archives of this transaction or of the price Alice paid for the Cransley estates. But it is possible to hazard a reasonable guess at the price from information available about the way in which Alice dealt with the property and what happened to it subsequently.

In view of her impending marriage Alice can never have intended to take up residence in Cransley. She bought the property with money inherited from her first husband, Henry Robinson, who left one third of his estate to Alice and another third to be divided equally between his surviving children on reaching full age or on marriage. Everything seems to point to the fact that the purchase was made from Alice's own inheritance; her purpose in any case was to divide the Cransley property equally between her surviving Robinson children. How the division was worked out is not very clear. From the only record which has survived it appears to have been made on the basis of a list of named fields, woods and other lands apportioned so that each share was roughly equivalent in total area. This must have made the individual shares difficult to manage, but it may be that some attempt was made to equalise the income, in the form of rents, coming from each share. One fifth passed to Margaret, who had married John Brett in 1591 (see Chapter 6). A second share went to Alice Robinson, who married John Washbourne at St Michael's Church in Bassishaw in February 1598. This is the only share of which details still exist; they are recorded on a map entitled 'Portion of Plan of Cransley Manor' and said to have been 'attached to the marriage settlement of Alice Robinson, December 1598.' The area of the property listed on this map is given as 394 acres.[4] The third share went to Anne who married Robert Rich, a barrister, in August 1599, also at St Michael's Church. Rich was the owner of five houses in Chancery Lane, where he lived, and was not interested in owning property in Cransley. So he sold his wife's share back to Alice Owen for the sum of £4,000.[5] If this represented the purchase price of one fifth of the Cransley estates – and one must assume that he did not try to take a profit from his mother-in-law – it suggests that the amount paid to Thomas Cecil in 1595 for the whole property was £20,000, a considerable sum at that time, representing an average of £10 an acre.

The fourth share was allocated to Alice's other son, John, but he sadly died in 1597 at the age of 14 and it reverted to his mother. Henry, who thus became the only Robinson son and heir, received the fifth share, to which his mother added John's share and the share repurchased from Robert Rich. So by 1600 Henry, then aged 14, was possessed of three-fifths of the Cransley Manors and lands, amounting to some 1,200 acres.

Henry was to become the first Robinson of Cransley. Nothing is known of his early years, though it can be taken for granted that Alice would have wished to give him a good education. Given her close connection with the Mercers, it is possible that he may have attended St Paul's School. But there were by the end of the century a number of London grammar schools from which to choose. Perhaps a more likely supposition, in the case of someone of her standing and wealth, is that she employed a tutor to teach first John and then Henry in her own home. The curriculum, wherever taught, would have included Grammar, which meant Latin, arithmetic and geometry and skills in argument and debate, through study of 'logic' and 'rhetoric'. All this would have continued until the age of about fifteen. What happened after that? He was not apprenticed in either the Brewers' or the Mercers' Company. Nor is he listed as an undergraduate of either Oxford or Cambridge University, and he had no training as a lawyer. So it is reasonable to suggest that he applied himself to learning something about the management of the Cransley estate which he was destined to take over, and possibly with his mother's help to renovating the house left by Thomas Cecil. The next certain fact known about him is his marriage, in July 1611, at the age of 25 to Mary Glover, daughter of the late Sir William Glover. A fuller account of the marriages of the Robinson children is given in Chapter 10.

Meanwhile Alice had taken steps to acquire that other prerequisite for 'gentility', a coat of arms. Her request to the College of Arms was granted in December 1595, nine months after her marriage to Thomas Owen, in her maiden name of Wilkes. The grant is recorded as having been made to: 'Alice Wilkes daughter of Thomas Wilkes wife to Judge Owen first married to Alderman Elkin'. For some reason she omitted to include any reference to her marriage to Henry Robinson. Details of the grant and the blazon are given in Appendix C. So she had achieved her goal! This will certainly have been gratifying to Alice. The grant was of course personal to her, it brought with it no retrospective or collateral rights or significance. So the Wilkes family arms began and ended with Alice and could not be inherited by her Wilkes nephews. But the fact that she was now armigerous strengthened her claim to the honorary title of 'Dame' which history has accorded to her and which was perpetuated in the name of the school she founded.

It is now time to go back to Thomas Owen and his origins and marriage to Alice. The story of Cransley after Alice's death is continued in Chapter 12.

Chapter 8

The Owens of Machynlleth, Shrewsbury and Lincoln's Inn

Alice's third husband, Thomas Owen, came from a very different background from either Henry Robinson or William Elkin. Thomas, a friend and neighbour, was much the most distinguished of Alice's husbands whose known Welsh ancestry stretched back for well over 600 years. Although she was married to him for a little less than four years, it is under the name of Owen that her fame has been perpetuated to this day, so it would seem appropriate to devote some time to an account of Thomas's Welsh origins and his life and career prior to his marriage to Alice.

Thomas Owen's 14 times great-grandfather, in the male line of descent, was Edwin ap Grono, Prince of Tegaingle, who in 1040 was living in Llanergan (now called Northop in County Flint).[1] Founder of the '12th Royal Tribe of Wales', he married the daughter of the King of Powys and was killed in one of the many internecine feuds pursued in the wild country to the west of Offa's Dyke. This border between England and Wales was guarded on the English side by the equally unruly Marcher Barons – said to number some 140 – established by William the Conqueror and installed in castle strongholds stretching from Mold in the north to Monmouth in the south.[2]

In the 12th century Edwin's great-grandson, Llewellyn ap Idnerth, came to live in Machynlleth, then a small town on the west coast of Powys. Within a hundred years Machynlleth had become a prosperous market centre and port serving the surrounding country, with a wide range of craftsmen and merchants, and had established trading links with Shrewsbury and Oswestry for its wool, cloth, hides and other products. The town is famous in Welsh history as the seat of the first Welsh parliament convened by Owen Glendower, himself a returned expatriate from England, who was the leader of the successful, though shortlived, uprising against the English at the beginning of the 15th century.

It was not until the late 15th century that the Welsh people recognised in Henry Tudor (Henry VII) a King of England who was one of their own countrymen. It was his son, Henry VIII, who finally united the two countries in 1536 under the Act of Union which incorporated Wales in the English parliamentary and administrative system. Henceforth justice was rigorously administered under the strengthened authority of the Council in the Marches, which exercised jurisdiction throughout Wales and the border counties.

Meanwhile, Llewellyn ap Idnerth's descendants remained in Machynlleth as well-to-do merchants, until the time of Thomas Owen's grandfather, Owen ap Griffith. His wife, Gwenwhyfar, was the daughter of Thomas Ireland, a member of a prominent family of merchants in Shrewsbury and Oswestry, but her given name left no doubt of her Welsh blood. Their son, Richard, born in Machynlleth in the last decade of the 15th century, migrated to Shrewsbury. He probably served an apprenticeship there, but in any case he was admitted as a Burgess or 'freeman' of Shrewsbury by purchase (at the price of £2 10s.) in 1520. This made him a member of the Commons, or Corporation, with certain privileges including freedom to trade and participation in the selection of Shrewsbury's two members of Parliament.

By 1530 Burgesses numbered 230, about half of all male householders. It was probably at this point that Richard abandoned the Welsh patronymic prefix 'ap' and adopted Owen as the family surname, an example followed by others of the family who followed him from Machynlleth during the 16th century and, in many cases, became prominent in Shrewsbury. He became a freeman of the Mercers' Company of Shrewsbury in 1523,[3] and he probably did pursue business as a Mercer. The Mercers and Drapers were the two leading companies among the 16 craft-fellowships in Shrewsbury at the time. Unlike their more prestigious counterparts, the Livery Companies of London, membership of the Shrewsbury companies was not limited to a single trade. They were in effect amalgamations of a wide variety of different and not obviously related trades.

The Mercers, for example, included ironmongers, goldsmiths, pewterers, apothecaries, upholsterers, stationers and others.[4] The Drapers, of which Richard's nephew Edward Owen was to become a prosperous member, included wool and cloth merchants and, more surprisingly, brewers. Richard married Mary Ottley in 1531, whose family were prominent wool merchants, also Drapers. These families – Owen, Ireland, Ottley – with a handful of others were the civic leaders in a town which was growing rapidly in size and importance in the 16th century, no longer as a frontier stronghold but as a regional market serving the needs of the neighbouring counties of England and Wales with the products of its own craftsmen as well as being a major centre for processing materials from Welsh towns such as Machynlleth, pre-eminently wool and cloth, and for their onward despatch to London. From 3,000 in the first half of the century the population doubled by 1600, and the solid magnificence of the mansions built during this period is witness to the wealth derived from this expanding trade, as well as from the upsurge in litigation which inevitably accompanied it and which lined the pockets of the town's lawyers.

This was the Shrewsbury in which, in the parish of St Chad, Thomas Owen, the eldest son of Richard and Mary, was born about 1540.[5] Three other sons followed, Richard, Robert and John, at short intervals and a daughter, Elizabeth. Richard senior was the first of the Owen family to settle in Shrewsbury and bring up a family there. One half-brother, by his father's first wife, Isabel, remained in Machynlleth and his descendants were the Owens of Bettws in

Powys; in the next generation, the family of another half-brother moved to Shrewsbury and, like Thomas and his brothers, played a prominent role in the public life of the town. They clearly all maintained their connections with the family in Wales, and they must have come to know well the sixty-odd miles of road between Shrewsbury and Machynlleth, running through Welshpool and under the shadow of the great mountains of Snowdonia. This would have been at least a two days' journey by horseback and the road passed by properties owned by the family in Powys and Montgomery.

Nothing is known about the early education of Richard Owen's family, except that it took place in Shrewsbury. They may have gone to a 'petty school' – some took girls as well as boys – from age five onwards, where they would have learned reading, writing and elementary arithmetic. Or they may have been educated by a private tutor, which a rich merchant's family could well afford, perhaps combining with the children of other merchants in the town. The boys would need these accomplishments before moving on at eight or nine, almost certainly to the Grammar School in Shrewsbury, for admission to which their father, as a Burgess, would have benefited from a reduced charge of four pence. As the Grammar School did not admit girls, at this stage Elizabeth's education would have been taken over by her mother. Life at the Grammar School was hard. The day's work began at six in the morning and continued until five in the evening on six days in the week, with a break for lunch and two vacations of about two weeks each at Christmas and Easter. Latin was the main subject studied, in the form of language and literature. Boys were required to speak Latin to one another outside lessons, and there were penalties for breaking this rule. This was the language needed for many official purposes, an essential tool still for many professions even in the mid-16th century. Besides Latin the study of the scriptures was an important subject but, except for arithmetic, not much else.

At the age of 16 Thomas went up to Oxford. He matriculated and was admitted as a student at Christ Church (the college founded by Cardinal Wolsey early in the century) in November 1556. He also had some connection with Broadgates Hall, an academic hall which was later absorbed into Pembroke College when the latter was founded in 1624. This hall had recently come into the possession of Christ Church on the dissolution of St Frideswide's Priory, and it may be that it was his place of residence while he was studying at Christ Church.[6] There had been a major change at Oxford during the first half of the 16th century. Previously the universities had catered primarily for scholars, often from poor homes, who were destined for life in the service of the Church or perhaps to serve the state in some minor capacity. Now Oxford and Cambridge had opened their doors to admit 'gentlemen commoners', as fee-paying undergraduates. These were the sons of noblemen, of gentlemen and professional men and of rich merchants who increasingly took advantage of the benefits, or in some cases the cachet, of acquiring a university degree. This had its downside: the new undergraduates had money to spend, and among them were a number who sought to combine the minimum of work with the maximum of pleasure. Hasn't it always been thus? But at this time it was a relatively new experience and the universities' reputations suffered. William Harrison wrote that 'they ruffle and roist it out, exceeding in apparel and riotous company ... . And for excuse, when charged with the breach of all good order, think it sufficient to say that they be gentlemen', as if that were a complete justification.[7] The great benefit of the change in admission policy, which outweighed the downside, was that it produced a new class of educated public servants and professional men who were appointed to fill the great offices of state on the basis of their ability and qualifications rather than just their birth. Such were William Cecil and Francis Walsingham, both educated at Cambridge; and Thomas Egerton (a future Lord Chancellor) who was a friend and contemporary of Thomas Owen at Oxford and subsequently at Lincoln's Inn.

The traditional medieval curriculum remained virtually unchanged in the middle of the century. It was based on the 'Trivium' of Grammar (meaning Latin), Rhetoric (involving participation in debates in Latin) and Dialectics (the study of logic, embodying principles derived from Aristotle); and the 'Quadrivium' of arithmetic, geometry, astronomy and music. Besides the general study of Latin texts, subjects were taught by lecturers (often of indifferent standard); formal debates ('Disputations'); and oral presentations ('Declarations'). For the serious student this was a crowded syllabus to cover adequately in four years. Thomas survived it and went down in 1560 having gained his Bachelor's degree in the previous year. He did not stay the additional three years required for a Master's degree, because he had by then decided to train as a lawyer. He had a two years' gap before starting at Lincoln's Inn and it is not known where he spent this time. Thomas was, like many of his educated contemporaries, a considerable linguist, so perhaps he spent these two years improving his language skills. He would certainly have spoken Welsh from his childhood and was fluent in Latin. He spoke French, which he would have needed, in the form of 'Law-French', in his future professional life, and he was evidently able to read and converse in Spanish and Italian, to judge from the books in these languages which he kept in his library.

Thomas's legal training began in 1562. He started at Fumival's Inn, one of the two 'Inns of Chancery' (the other being Thavies Inn) attached to Lincoln's Inn at which students spent the first two years of their training (the Inns of Chancery, of which there were 10 serving the four Inns of Court, have long disappeared). Fumival's was in Holborn, only a short walk from Lincoln's Inn in Chancery Lane, whose senior members supervised the studies. Lincoln's Inn had strong Shropshire and Welsh connections, which made it the obvious choice for Thomas, and of the four Inns of Court was the least resistant to the Protestant reforms and the Act of Uniformity.

Law students, like their Oxford counterparts, had the reputation for being an unruly crowd, and for similar reasons. Many members admitted to the Inns had no intention of following a legal career. A spell at an Inn was regarded as much a part of a gentleman's education as going up to Oxford, and for those intent on enjoying the pleasures and vices of London life there was a lot to spend money on, more indeed than at either Oxford or Cambridge. Even the normal expenses of fees, required costume and dinners, virtually precluded the entry of poor men's sons. This is not to suggest that more serious students eschewed the many benefits of the cultural life of London, though it was a bit early for playgoing which later became their successors' favourite diversion. But for Thomas, and other aspiring barristers, the work was hard and unremitting, especially for students of Common Law, which has been described as 'a formless, confused jumble of undigested particulars, successfully resisting all efforts at simplification or systematic structure.'[8] This sounds enough to put anyone off starting! The formidable task of learning and digesting the reports of Common Law cases, an essential discipline, was somewhat less daunting for those, like Thomas Owen, who had already had the grounding of an Oxford education. As Owen was to discover, it was worthwhile, since Common Law, which was concerned with all property and civil disputes between individuals, was, in a highly litigious age, the busiest and also the most lucrative field in which to be involved.

And 'confused jumble' though it may have been, one contemporary at least described it in different terms. Writing in the reign of James I, he said: 'Whatsoever is not disagreeing from the law of God and is consonent to the law of nature and nations, allowed by the custom of our country, is the undoubted common law of this realm, which acknowledgeth no other author but God and Nature.'[9] The author was none other than Sir Roger Owen, Thomas Owen's son.

While this does not invalidate the definition quoted above, neither is inconsistent with a more recent judgement that English Common-Law 'was perhaps the most significant achievement of mediaeval England.'[10]

The legal year consisted (as it still does) of four terms; in addition there were two 'learning vacations' in Lent and August. Much of the learning involved endless reading, as well as regular whole day debates on hypothetical cases involving controversial points of law, and observing the courts in action at Westminster Hall. On completion of his initial two years Thomas entered Lincoln's Inn as an 'Inner Barrister', the lowest rung of the legal ladder. He must have made his mark since, in 1564, he was appointed Principal of Furnival's Inn. This was evidently not a very happy position as he seems to have become involved in an acrimonious dispute with his fellow-members over the running of the Inn, which was brought before a disciplinary hearing of the Benchers (see below). It was settled by what looks like a drawn game, both sides being criticised but neither severely. Lincoln's Inn contained about 160 junior members in Thomas's time. It took a further six years, the normal period of training, before he was called to the Bar as 'Utter Barrister', in June 1570, at the same time as his friend, Thomas Egerton, though the latter was required to 'bringe certificate from the Basshoppe that he is reconsiled in Religion'[11] before his promotion was confirmed, a possible indication of doubt about his or his family's acceptance of the Act of Uniformity. (This had special significance following the Pope's excommunication of Queen Elizabeth in the preceding February.)

As an 'Utter (or Outer) Barrister', one of 60 or so at Lincoln's Inn, he was qualified to undertake legal work; after a further five years he became an 'apprentice at law', with the right to plead at any court in the country except the Court of Common Pleas, which remained the exclusive preserve of the 'Serjeants at Law.' The Government of the Inn was run by the 'Benchers', a select body of some 20 senior barristers. Owen and Thomas Egerton both became Benchers in November 1579.

The Benchers made the rules for conduct of members of the Inn and imposed penalties for infringement. The rules were many and varied. Some examples will give their flavour: shooting with bows and arrows was not permitted; attendance at daily service in Chapel was compulsory; members must not wear their shirts outside their doublets; they must not speak 'loude and hype' at meal times, nor provoke quarrels; nor were they permitted to entertain women in their chambers, and anyone caught fornicating in his chamber was fined £5, though this was reduced to £1 if the offence took place in the garden or in Chancery Lane! Drunkenness as such was not punished, perhaps because it was too prevalent to do anything about. In practice the Benchers' writ ran only within the purlieus of the Inn itself; no attempt was made to regulate personal behaviour outside the Inn, except possibly in the case of dress. This varied according to rank. Junior members wore a sleeveless gown and black cloth cap; barristers a long black robe with velvet welts on the sleeves; and benchers a knee-length gown tufted with silk and velvet, with a velvet cap. The first two ranks were forbidden to wear their gowns outside the Inn, but this may have been intended to avoid clashes with the townspeople.[12]

Once called to the Bar, Thomas Owen did not wait long for employment. At the end of June 1570 he was asked to arbitrate in a dispute between Alderman Lionel Duckett and a fellow Mercer. Duckett had been Master of the Mercers' Company in 1566 and was to be again in 1571 and twice thereafter. The illustration shows him wearing his Alderman's scarlet gown and the livery of the Mercers' Company. As Master in 1571 Duckett sponsored Owen for admission as a Freeman of the Mercers' Company by Redemption, without payment of the customary 'fine' (fee), a signal honour for a young man. This was the start of Owen's connection with the Mercers which was to last for the rest of his life. Duckett had recently married Jane Baskerville, widow of Humphrey Baskerville, who had been Master of the Mercers' Company in 1559 and who died in 1564. This too had an important effect on Thomas's future, as will be seen below.

Baskerville was an interesting character. He was a brave man of strong principle, as he had shown when a member of the jury at the trial in 1554 of Sir Nicholas Throckmorton, who was accused of taking part in the rebellion of Sir Thomas Wyatt, the object of which was to depose Queen Mary. Wyatt was executed and it was expected that, accused by the Crown of high treason and under a Catholic judge, Throckmorton would suffer a like fate. But he exercised his right to object to the original jury, presumably because of their known Catholic sympathies, and Baskerville, a staunch Protestant whose wife, Jane, was a member of the well-known reforming family of Packington, was appointed to the new jury. This jury was packed with like-minded reformers, possibly chosen by the known Protestant Sheriff. After lengthy deliberation the jury acquitted Throckmorton, to the fury of the Queen who imprisoned all the members for eight months, but found it impossible to take any further action against them. Throckmorton went on to pursue a successful, though by no means trouble-free, career until his death in 1571. Baskerville evidently suffered no ill consequences, and served as Sheriff and Alderman in Queen Elizabeth's reign.[13]

This diversion on Baskerville is a prelude to recording that his daughter, Sarah, was married to Thomas Owen in 1572. Sarah was by then the step-daughter of Lionel Duckett and the marriage took place in the year in which Duckett was Mayor of London. Her brother, also Humphrey Baskerville, had been admitted to the Freedom of the Mercers' Company by patrimony in the previous year, so this was one more link with the Mercers for Owen. Thomas and Sarah's first child, Roger, was born in September 1573, and in this year too Sarah's step-father was knighted. At a period when the prospects of success depended as much on connections as on ability, Thomas Owen had taken the first steps on the path to a prominent and profitable legal career. Networking was as much a feature of life in the 16th century as it is in the 21st; and correct religious sympathies were even more important as a means not only to preferment but also to ensuring security of tenure.

Chapter 9

Judge Owen

Not long after his marriage Thomas Owen bought a house in Basinghall Street in the London Ward of Bassishaw, which remained his home for the rest of his life. This move probably took place at the end of 1573 or early 1574. William Elkin, whose connections with Owen through the Mercers' Company have been noted in Chapter 6, also owned a house in Bassishaw, to which he probably moved at the end of the decade. Alice Robinson came to live there on her marriage to him in 1586, so the Owens and Elkins were near neighbours.

Bassishaw, also known as Basinghall, was – and is – the smallest of the 26 Wards of the City of London. In the 16th century it consisted of one street, Basinghall Street, and also included the back gate to the Guildhall and part of the building, the principal part, however, being in the Cheap Ward, which adjoined Bassishaw to the south. (The whole Guildhall is now in Bassishaw.) Unlike other City Wards which boasted at least three or four churches, Bassishaw had only one, St Michael's, of 14th-century origin, at the north end of Basinghall Street, which was burned down in the fire of 1666, rebuilt and finally demolished in 1897. Near the south end of the street were two other churches: to the east St Stephen's, in Coleman Street Ward, since destroyed; and to the west, St Lawrence Jewry, in Cheap Ward beside the Guildhall, which is still in active use. All three churches were associated with key events in the lives of Thomas and Alice.

Basinghall Street ran then, virtually as it does now, from London Wall in the north to Cateaton Street (now Gresham Street) in the south. The principal building was Bakewell Hall (also called Blackwell Hall) at the south end, which had been for many years the main London market for woollen cloth. It was to this market that the Shrewsbury merchants sent their cloth and from here that English cloth was exported to the staple at Antwerp or Calais. During Thomas Owen's time, the old Hall was pulled down and a new warehouse built.

According to Stow, the Hall was originally owned by the Bassing family, from which the street and Ward took their name, at least early in the 13th century, but was probably in the hands of the Bakewells by the middle of the 14th century, before being adopted as a cloth market.[1] The Weavers' Company had their hall in Basinghall Street, and the Masons, the Coopers and the Girdlers also had halls there. None of these buildings has survived, and only the Girdlers still have their hall in Bassishaw today.

Along the rest of Basinghall Street, mainly at the southern end, were in Stow's words 'divers fair houses for merchants and others'. None of these remain; many were destroyed in the Great Fire of 1666 or demolished to make way for modem buildings. In Thomas's time they would, mostly, have been narrow-fronted on the street side, three or four storeys high, timber-framed with lath and plaster panels between the timbers and with upper storeys jettied over the ground floor. The full depth of the house, behind the narrow face, may have contained as many as three rooms on each floor. The rooms would have been heated by open fires, burning by this time sea-coal, conveyed by ship from the coal mines in the north of the country, and the smoke from the fires now removed by tall chimneys. By the second half of the 16th century those rich enough to afford such houses would have filled the rectangular window frames with glass in diagonal panes. This meant that, during daytime, the rooms were reasonably well lit, though after dark tallow candles must have made them fairly gloomy, except on special occasions when candles in wall brackets and self-standing candelabras were lighted in the great chamber or other room used for receptions and entertaining. Houses of this size required a large staff of servants, probably more than a dozen in all, including the principal ones such as a steward or chamberlain, valet or page, chambermaid or lady's maid and cook. It is unlikely that Thomas and Sarah started their married life quite at this level but this is the sort of household they would have aspired to as Thomas's abilities became recognised and rewarded, an aspiration which was evidently soon to be realised. William Elkin, moving to Bassishaw with his first wife some years later at a time when he was already at the peak of his profession, would also have lived in a house of this kind.

The Owens' eldest son, Roger, was baptised in September 1573 at St Stephen's, Coleman Street, the church at which Sarah's father, Humphrey Baskerville, was buried. The newly-married couple may have been living with Sarah's mother and step-father, Sir Lionel Duckett, at the time; this was common practice at the period for a young mother awaiting her first child. Sir Lionel, who was in the year of his Mayoralty, was a local resident and Alderman for Bassishaw from 1567 until his death in 1587.

Thomas and Sarah's next children were twins, Thomas and Jane. They were baptised in October 1574 at St Michael's, Bassishaw as were their further seven children. These were Margaret (born 1575), Richard and Elizabeth (1577), William (1581), Sarah (1582) and Mary (1587). All, except possibly Roger, were born in their house in Basinghall Street. All five sons and five daughters survived their mother and their father. In this respect Sarah was more fortunate, perhaps unusually so for the age, than Alice, of whose 11 children by her first husband, Henry Robinson, all born during exactly the same period as Sarah's, only four survived infancy or early childhood.

After he was called to the Bar, work soon began to come Thomas's way. The Mercers' connection paid off; he was engaged in several cases during the 1570s and thereafter was employed by the Company on numerous occasions throughout the rest of his career. Another source of briefs was the Privy Council, which made frequent demands on his services from 1577 onwards. No doubt his wife's family connections as well as his own sympathies helped to promote his interests here; the story of Humphrey Baskerville's defiance of Queen Mary has been told in Chapter 8 and Sarah's mother, Jane, came from a leading reforming family, the Packingtons. It would not be surprising that a promising young barrister with this background should have come to the notice of William Cecil, who had been out of office and out of favour during Queen Mary's reign owing to his Protestant sympathies. After being Chief Secretary to Queen Elizabeth until 1572, he was now, as Lord Burghley, Lord High Treasurer and the most influential member of the Privy Council.

The breadth of the Common Law is shown by the great diversity of cases remitted to Owen by the Privy Council. For example, he dealt with a petition from a seaman's wife, examined the causes of a riot in London and numerous charges of corruption, coining false money and rape, and handled the deportation of a 'lewd and unreverent' Walloon. He had the unsavoury task of questioning several traitors under torture. And in 1588 he was one of the 16 lawyers instructed to consider the repeal or amendment of certain Parliamentary Statutes relating to legal matters.[2] Following his election as a Bencher in 1579, Owen also held several appointments at Lincoln's Inn. His first was as Reader in 1583, an onerous task involving supervision of the training of the students and recommending those qualified to be called to the Bar; then in 1586 he was 'Keeper of the Black Book', the record of the proceedings of the Council of Benchers for Lincoln's Inn which dates from 1422; and finally he was Treasurer of the Inn in 1588, a position of special honour.

His promotion to the rank of Serjeant-at-Law came in 1589, in honour of which the Lincoln's Inn Benchers graciously presented him with £10 and a pair of 'Oxford' gloves. This was a Royal appointment made by writ under the Great Seal; those appointed are often referred to as having been raised to the 'degree of the Coif', so-called after the close-fitting white silk cap which was the symbol of their rank, together with a gown of mulberry and gold stripes. This appointment was roughly equivalent to 'taking silk' today. The rank of King's Counsel (now Queen's Counsel) to which this term applies originated in the early 17th century and had long overtaken in prestige that of Serjeant-at-Law before the latter was abolished in 1877.

Serjeants-at-Law neither resided in nor took direct part in the government of their Inn of Court, though their connections remained close and their influence strong. Instead they became members of one of the two Serjeants' Inns, in Fleet Street and Chancery Lane. Owen joined the former, of which he became one of the 'lessees' in 1592. As a Serjeant-at-Law, he was entitled to appear before the judges of the Court of Common Pleas, the principal Court for dealing with personal civil cases, many of them appeals from the lower Courts in county centres.

The right to plead in this Court remained, until 1846, the exclusive pre-serve of Serjeants; barristers who had not attained this rank could appear at all Courts in the country except for this one. The Court sat in Westminster Hall, the only surviving part of the original Royal Palace of the Norman and Angevin kings, which had been the home of the Law Courts since the 13th century (and remained so until the building of the Law Courts in the Strand in the late 19th century). The Court of Common Pleas was located on the right-hand side of the Hall near the entrance at the north end. The layout was very simple. The Judges sat on raised benches, 27 feet long, with their clerks below them, the barristers and litigants sat on plain planks on either side and in the centre were trestle tables. This was the busiest and slowest court of civil jurisdiction applying Common Law in relation to contracts and person-to-person cases, presided over by its own Chief Justice. It also occupied the coldest and draughtiest position in the Hall until it was moved to more suitable premises in the 18th century.

The discomfort to which Common Pleas was subjected looks suspiciously like jealousy on the part of the other two Courts which occupied the best positions at the south end of the Hall. The first, on the left-hand side, was the Court of the King's Bench, with the Chief Justice of England presiding, which dealt primarily with criminal cases but which increasingly in the 16th century asserted the right to exercise jurisdiction in civil cases in deliberate rivalry to the Court of Common Pleas. The second, on the opposite side, was the Court of Chancery, the Lord Chancellor's court of civil jurisdiction, in which the developing principles of equity law were applied. In practice this court too, which also dealt with petitions, must often have encroached on the functions of the Court of Common Pleas at a time when the distinctions between equity and the Common Law were still not clearly established. On the first floor sat the Court of the Star Chamber, so-called from the decor of the room in which it met, consisting of Privy Councillors. This was, in effect, the Lord Chancellor's criminal court, with wide jurisdiction over all matters capable of leading to a breach of the peace. Large though the Westminster Hall is, the noise and confusion when several courts were in session at the same time must have been formidable.[3]

Active though his professional life in London was, Thomas Owen kept up his close connections with Shrewsbury. Travel between London and Shrewsbury, a distance of about 160 miles, was neither fast nor, given the state of the roads, comfortable. But it has been reckoned that 'going at a steady pace on horseback, men with business in London could reach the capital in four days.[4] This was a journey which Owen, along with many of his contemporaries, was evidently prepared, and required, to make fairly frequently.

He became a Justice of the Peace for Shropshire in 1583. This was a Crown appointment held by prominent county gentlemen, nominated by the Lord Lieutenant. Justices of the Peace were unpaid and so, to a degree, independent. But as they had to be reappointed annually, their independence was somewhat limited by the fact that no one wanted to suffer the indignity of non-renewal. JPs were in effect the backbone of local administration and law enforcement, under the general oversight of the Privy Council. They were responsible for such diverse matters as the licensing of ale-houses, regulating the status of apprentices, enforcing the poor law, setting local rates and, a duty not always scrupulously exercised, the upkeep of roads, bridges and prisons.

Among their number were included some barristers with local connections, such as Thomas Owen, whose legal advice was of particular value at the County Quarter Sessions at which the JPs sat; these were nominally held in Ludlow but sometimes, in the second half of the 16th century, in Shrewsbury. But many of their administrative and quasi-judicial functions were exercised in their own manor houses throughout the county. They had wide jurisdiction in criminal cases, described as 'felonies' (for which they were able to impose the death penalty where prescribed), though the most serious ones were remitted to the Assizes, held twice a year in Shrewsbury by two senior judges on circuit from the central courts in London. These were major events, social as well as judicial, accompanied by public celebrations and great ceremony. At a later stage in his career (see below) this was a duty that Owen had to perform.

About the same time, Thomas's eldest son, Roger, began his final education in Shrewsbury. He was admitted to Shrewsbury School in November 1584 at the age of eleven.[5] This school was founded in 1552, financed by contributions from the rich merchant community and by the 1580s was probably the largest grammar school in England with between 400 and 500 boys. It was popular with families of the gentry throughout Shropshire and north Wales, as well as of merchants living in the town, but, not surprisingly in the 16th century, the mix between the two classes was not always harmonious. Like all schools, it came under ecclesiastical jurisdiction and required a licence from the Bishop. To obtain this the school had to guarantee a minimum standard of behaviour by its masters: the statutes laid down that they were not to be 'common gamesters, nor common haunters of the taverns or alehouses or other suspect houses',[6] and the Headmaster's salary, at £40 a year, was the highest in the country.[7]

Whether Thomas maintained a house in Shrewsbury is not known. But in any case his cousin Edward Owen, a Draper who was four times Bailiff, built Bellstone Hall in 1582 and Thomas's younger brother Richard, also a Draper, was in business in Shrewsbury and built Owen's Mansion in 1592, and so no doubt Roger would have boarded with one of his relatives.[8] Discipline was quite as severe and the hours of work just as long as in Thomas's schooldays (see Chapter 8) and there had been little change in the curriculum, except that translations of Latin authors were more readily available and acceptable. Roger followed his father at Christ Church, Oxford and obtained a Bachelor's degree in 1592. By that time he had already been admitted to Lincoln's Inn, where he was called to the Bar in 1597.

As Roger started at school in 1584, Thomas was elected to Parliament as one of the two Burgesses representing Shrewsbury. Out of a total electorate of 420, being the number of Burgesses all entitled to the vote, he secured 366 votes, against 299 for the second elected representative and 176 for a third contender. He was one of 53 lawyers in a House of Commons of 460 members, of whom 78 were Knights of the Shires, that is to say, county representatives, and most of the remainder representatives of the Boroughs. The House sat from November 1584 until March 1585, longer than the average of 10 weeks for sessions following the 10 elections which took place in Queen Elizabeth's reign. It met in St Stephen's Chapel (in the Westminster Palace) to which it had removed from the Abbey Chapterhouse in 1548 and which remained its meeting place until destroyed by fire in 1834. (Its replacement on the same site was bombed in 1941 and the rebuilt Houses of Parliament were first used in 1950.)

The opening of this Parliament, the only one of which Owen was a member, was a splendid occasion. The High Officers of State and of the judiciary together with the members of the House of Lords – 65 peers and 26 bishops – all in their robes took part in the procession from St James's Palace first to Westminster Abbey for a service and sermon and then to the Chamber of the Upper House, in Westminster Palace. The Queen wearing her 'imperial robes' and a gold coronet travelled in a litter carried between two white horses. In the Chamber, which was on the first floor above a large vault on the ground floor, the judges and the Royal Councillors sat on two large woolsacks covered with red cloth, forming two sides of a square, with the Queen's throne and seats for the Lord Chancellor and the Lord Keeper of the Great Seal on the third side, and the Clerks of Parliament and of the Crown on the fourth. Behind the woolsacks were benches for members of the Upper House and behind on the side facing the Queen a rail in front of an open space where the Commons stood, headed by the Speaker, on being summoned by the Lords. Members of the House of Commons each swore the Oath of Supremacy according to the Act of 1563, administered by the Lord Steward, before answering the summons and hearing brief words of welcome from the Queen. These were followed by the 'Queen's Speech', in those days read by the Lord Keeper. As at the opening of every Parliament, the speech included confirmation of members' right to freedom of speech and immunity from arrest, but accompanied by warnings against abuse. The Commons then turned to their daily business much of which centred round religion, taxation and arguments about the 'prerogative.'[9]

In fact, short though the session was, a great deal of other business was evidently transacted. During his single session as MP, Owen sat on committees concerned with ecclesiastical livings, the maintenance of the navy, fraudulent conveyances, delays in executions and the good government of the City of Westminster, a full portfolio for a short period.[10] MPs were unpaid but they were able to claim 'expenses' of four shillings a day for Knights of the Shire and two shillings for Burgesses, including travelling time to and from their constituencies. These payments were levied by the Sheriffs on the counties and by the Boroughs' authorities for the Burgesses, but many MPs did not draw their entitlement. It may be surmised that Owen was among the latter.

This was the extent of Owen's short career as a Member of Parliament. He did not stand again in 1586. By then he was heavily involved in commitments on behalf of the Privy Council and the Mercers, and in his duties at Lincoln's Inn, which have already been mentioned. But affairs in Shropshire also absorbed much of his time.

In 1586 he acquired the Manor of Condover, with its medieval manor house, about six miles south of Shrewsbury. More will be said about this venture below. Then in 1588, the year before he became a Serjeant-at-Law, Owen was appointed as Recorder of Shrewsbury. This was a specially appropriate appointment, given his and his family's close connection with the town, and would have given him great pleasure. His judicial functions as Recorder involved presiding when required at the Quarter Sessions held in Shrewsbury. But he was also the town's principal legal officer. In this capacity he acted as adviser to the town authorities and was often called upon to arbitrate in disputes between citizens or the merchant guilds. The principal town authorities were the two Bailiffs, who were elected annually by the Aldermen and Common Councillors. (They were replaced by a single Mayor in 1638.) They presided over the Small Court, which met weekly and exercised summary justice, or offered reconciliation where possible, and also over the Great Court, which met twice a year and on which male householders were selected to serve. These courts dealt with a wide range of civil offences, known as 'misdemeanours', many involving debt recovery, breach of contract, brawling or 'trespass', a term which then covered many forms of intrusion, and some felonies. The circumstances in which cases were, or could be, heard before a jury or referred to higher courts are complicated and have been well described elsewhere.[11] Suffice it to say that, since the Bailiffs and other town officials seldom had any training in the law, the Recorder's legal advice and experience were much in demand. During his time as Recorder, Owen was also made a member of the Council in the Marches (on the Council's functions, see Chapter 8), which had its headquarters in Ludlow Castle, although it also met in Shrewsbury, where some of its members, like Owen, lived and worked. The Council's relationship with the other courts is not very clear; it was empowered to hear both civil and criminal cases and also dealt with disputes arising from the conduct of Council elections. Clearly there was a good deal of overlapping. There is little evidence that Owen devoted much time to this appointment; indeed his busy schedule would hardly have allowed him to do so.

Owen completed his four-year term of office as Recorder in 1592. How often during this period he had to make the uncomfortable journey between Shrewsbury and London is impossible to tell. But he must have been frequently on the road in order to cope with his commitments to the Mercers, for whom he handled at least eight important cases in these four years, as well as discharging his duties as Treasurer of Lincoln's Inn. Sadly, his pleasure at gaining the Shrewsbury appointment was marred by the death of Sarah, his wife of 17 years, in London in August 1589, just two months before he took the oath as Serjeant.

On his return from Shrewsbury greater things were in store. He was selected as Queen's Serjeant for the year 1593-4. This was a highly prestigious

Royal appointment; one, or sometimes two, were made for each year. It may be imagined that his work for the Privy Council and contacts with the Cecils and other influential Councillors had resulted in his name being recommended to the Queen. His functions, during his year in office, were to represent the Crown's interests in Court and to act as the bearer of important communications and bills between the Lords and Commons. Clearly he performed these functions to the satisfaction of the Queen and her advisers, as he was appointed Judge of the Court of Common Pleas in January 1594. On his elevation to the Bench, he took precedence, together with Judges of the King's Bench, immediately after Peers of the Realm, Knights, Bishops, the Principal Officers of State and the Lords Chief Justice.

Just before him in precedence was his friend Thomas Egerton, who had been knighted in 1593 and elevated to the Bench as Master of the Rolls in the following year. Egerton, who was to become a distinguished Lord Chancellor (as Lord Ellesmere) in King James I's reign, was a great favourite of Queen Elizabeth. It is said that her independent decisions on his successive promotions irritated Lord Burghley. But this did not affect his friendship with Owen, who asked Egerton, and so recorded it in his Will in 1598, to be 'overseer' of his Will and 'patron' of his children. For undertaking these tasks, Egerton, who was by then Lord Keeper of the Great Seal, was to receive a legacy of £20.

His home in London remained in Bassishaw and it can be taken for granted that the Owens and Elkins were not only neighbours but also close friends. They may well have joined forces for the early education of their sons and daughters. After Sarah Owen died in 1589, it would have been natural for Alice Elkin to help in practical ways with the care and upbringing of the five Owen girls, who matched, age for age, so closely with Alice's four daughters from her two marriages; the eldest, Jane Owen, was then aged 15 and the youngest, Ursula Elkin, aged two. Two were soon off their respective families' hands. Jane Owen was married in December 1590, at the age of 16, at St Michael's Church. Her husband was Bonham Norton, of the well-known printing family, who held the patent for printing books on Common Law and was subsequently to become an Alderman, Master of the Stationers' Company and King's Printer to James I. Margaret Robinson's (second) marriage in May 1591 has already been recorded in Chapter 6.

When William Elkin died in 1593, his widow was no doubt glad to have a friend living close at hand to whom she could turn for advice and support. It has been suggested (in Chapter 7) that Thomas Owen helped Alice over her acquisition of the Cransley estate; almost certainly he will have advised her over her request for the grant of arms. So it is no great cause for surprise that Alice became Thomas's second wife and he her third husband just 16 months after William Elkin's death. Thomas and Alice signed a marriage settlement on 31 January 1595 and the marriage took place on 3 March at St Pancras, Soper Lane,[12] which was not a church or parish with which either of them appears to have had any previous connection. For some reason, they did not choose St Michael's, Bassishaw, or St Mary's, Islington, either of which would have been an obvious choice. St Pancras was the church at which William Elkin married his first wife in 1560; her children by her first husband were all baptised there and her home was in that parish. But this is no explanation for Thomas and Alice's decision to be married there!

With their large combined family, Alice and Thomas lived in his house in Basinghall Street. Elkin's house, which was not specifically mentioned in his Will (except to say that it was 'too little' for the dinner for the Lord Mayor and Aldermen which was to be paid for in his memory), was probably let and the proceeds became part of Alice's marriage settlement on her marriage to Thomas Owen.

It is time to return to Condover, which, as already mentioned, had come into Owen's life several years earlier. Condover had been a royal manor until the end of the 13th century; besides Condover itself, it included a number of small neighbouring villages. It was held by various families until the late 16th century when, in 1578, Thomas Owen jointly with Stephen Duckett, a relative of the London Mayor, acquired the lease. In 1586, after the death of the then Lord of the Manor, Owen purchased the freehold in his sole name. He immediately demolished the existing manor house and set about building a grand new Hall. Thomas was almost certainly responsible for its design. The profession of architect, in the modern sense, was unknown in the 16th century; it was only in the following century that it began to be recognised. So Thomas was in the company of such prominent contemporaries as William Cecil and Bess of Hardwick in applying their amateur talents to designing houses to suit their own ambitious requirements.

He employed a Master Mason to supervise the whole operation and it was from craftsmen such as this that professional architects developed. The project took a long time to fulfil. At the start tons of sandstone were delivered from local quarries; stone tiles and timber for the roof and floors were also obtained locally and the building provided employment for many local craftsmen for at least ten years. Only by 1598, the year of Thomas's death, could the Hall be said to be 'substantially complete' and even then there was evidently more work to be done by his son and heir, Roger.

The Hall has two storeys and a basement and is built of reddish sandstone on a typically Elizabethan H-shaped plan. It survives today very much in its original form. The manorial estate, when Owen purchased it, amounted to just over 1,400 acres in Condover parish, and included the advowson of the Church of St Andrew and St Mary. Only about 25 acres were kept as the 'home farm' by Owen, the rest being held by tenants. But Thomas and his successors added considerably to the size of the estate by purchases of neighbouring manors and farms, so that by early in the 17th century the total size must have been around 2,000 acres and the Park had been expanded to 300 acres.[13]

The rents from farms and other property on Owen's estates in Shropshire will have produced a considerable income. Added to this was the income from manorial estates in Wales inherited from his grandmother, and profits from a farming enterprise in Thurrock, Essex. As with many of his contemporaries, investments in these assets provided a valuable supplement to his professional income.

True to his age, Owen built his magnificent Hall at Condover in celebration of his material success. It reflected an ambition to leave as his memorial to future generations of his family a residence of which they could be proud. And it is probably not unjust to attribute to him a wish to surpass the grandeur of the mansions built in Shrewsbury by his brother and his cousin. What he could not have foreseen was the accolade awarded to him 350 years later by Nikolaus Pevsner's description of Condover Hall as 'the grandest Elizabethan house in Shropshire'.

Thomas certainly visited Shrewsbury regularly because of his close family and other connections in his capacity as circuit judge to preside at the Assizes. It was due to Thomas's influence and at his request that his son Roger was elected to the House of Commons in 1597 as one of the two Burgesses sent to represent Shrewsbury. The defeated candidate was none other than the Earl of Essex. It is unlikely that Thomas ever lived in Condover Hall, which was not fully completed by the time of his death. But he must have paid frequent visits to Condover to exercise supervision over the progress of the building in which he clearly took a close personal interest. Did Alice accompany him on these visits to Shropshire? There is no evidence to show whether she did or not. At the age of 48 it would not have been an easy journey for her and her family responsibilities in London were burdensome. But she was intrepid enough to undertake it and by the 1590s travel by carriage – of a sort – was beginning to become possible.

Life was busy for the Owens during their short marriage of 3½ years. Besides his duties at the Court of Common Pleas and on circuit, he was involved with various committees of the House of Lords. The records of some of his cases, in Law French, were published in 1650, with a preface eulogising his industry and authority, but the collection contains little of Owen's original work. In 1597 he was engaged by Lord Burghley to negotiate the settlement for the intended marriage of his granddaughter, Bridget de Vere, to the son and heir of the Earl of Pembroke. Bridget was the younger daughter of Burghley's poet and spendthrift son-in-law, the Earl of Oxford (whom some claim to have been the author of Shakespeare's plays). But the marriage never took place and Thomas had died by the time Bridget eventually did marry. In 1596 he was accorded a rare tribute by the Mercers' Company, who elected him as their Master for the following year, an unusual honour for someone who was not involved in the trade and had not served an apprenticeship in each of the three offices of Warden, which was the normal pre-condition for appointment as Master.

How much did Thomas Owen earn? One embittered contemporary observer complained that Common Lawyers were 'grown so great that no other sort dare meddle with them' and gave a figure of £20-30,000 for the annual income of Common Law judges and serjeants.[14] While this may be dismissed as a gross exaggeration inspired by jealousy, there is no doubt that the practice the conduct of the School and the appointment of the Master. It was finally decreed that the style of the foundations was to be 'The Free chapel and School of Alice Owen of London, Widow of Thomas Owen, in Islington, for the instruction of children'.[3]

The Master's house and School, combined in one building, were built at the south end of the row of Almshouses, with entrance directly from St John Street. The building was probably not completed until 1613 and the first Master, Mr William Leske (said to have been a friend of Alice's) was appointed early in that year, though it was not until late in the year that the School was opened for business. In her Will, made on 10 June 1613, Alice ordained:

> that my Executors and Supervisors of this my last Will and Testament shall sequester and take apart a Competent portion of my Estate for the purchasing of a parcell of ground of Twenty pounds yearly Rent that is not holden in Capite or in Chiefe for the maintenance of the Schoolmaster for the time present and others his successors either by me or my friends the Master and Wardens of the Company of Brewers of London (to whom after my decease I leave the Government of my Schoole) placed and elected to teach in my Schoole lately erected in the Parish of Clerkenwell in the County of Middlesex, if so be that before my Decease the said Ground be not purchased.

She went on to provide that, during any time which elapsed between her death and the purchase of the land, her Executors should pay the Schoolmaster the sum of five pounds a quarter; and an individual bequest of five pounds was also made to Mr Leske. This was a necessary provision because, as will be seen (in Chapter 12), the land was not acquired until several years after Alice's death.

Alice was meanwhile working on the Rules for the Almshouses and the School. There must have been some arrangements for admission of almswomen before 1613. But with the School due to open by the end of that year it was necessary to produce more formal Rules for both foundations. Alice is certain to have had her own views on what such Rules should say: the qualifications required for the Schoolmaster, the method of selecting the almswomen and scholars, the disciplines to be observed and the penalties for misbehaviour. She would need the help of a scrivener to transcribe her views into a set of workable rules and the advice of an attorney to ensure these were legally sound. All this took time and it was not until three months after the date of her Will that the document was completed, only a few days before her death. It was typical of her that her last concern should have been to get her wishes firmly established. They provide a revealing insight into the character and outlook of this woman, her caring nature, the obvious sincerity of her religious beliefs and her determination to create a disciplined but kindly regime for her beneficiaries.

The original Rules dated 1613 were subjoined to her Will. They were followed three days later by a Schedule of the annual expenditure on the two foundations, of which the titles follow the description of the various items in the Rules (described below). Unfortunately the original Rules have been detached from the Will and lost, though the Schedule remains. Several versions of the Rules or of extracts from them are extant. The most credible is a complete version written in the first person throughout, which is contained in an early 19th-century volume of documents held in Brewers' Hall. If this is not actually a true copy of the original it is certainly as close to it as it is now possible to get.[4]

In the preamble Alice records the 'nomination of my beloved and trusty friends the Master, Wardens and Commonalty of the Mystery or Art of Brewers of the City of London to be Governors, Rulers, Patrons and Maintainours' of the School and Almshouses. The first section contains orders for the School. The Schoolmaster is to be 'a single man and unmarried of honest life and good conversation', chosen, after her death, by the Brewers and approved by the Bishop of the Diocese. He would be given rent-free accommodation over the School House and porch and would receive wages of £5 a quarter. He should be able to teach 'grammar, fair writing, ciphering and casting of accounts, the better to train up young beginners whereby they may be fit to be apprentices or to take up some other honest course for the obtaining of their living.' He was not to absent himself from the School for more than 20 days in the year. He was not to indulge in 'gaming or haunting of ale houses and taverns' and could be expelled by the Governors for any serious offence, such as fornication, adultery, blasphemy, drunkenness or theft or for neglect or breach of any of the rules for the School. He was to be treated generously if he was unable to discharge his duties owing to sickness or age.

Thirty children (boys) were to be taught freely at the School, 24 from Islington and six from Clerkenwell. If any of them should be absent without the Schoolmaster's leave or through sickness for more than 30 days in the year he should be expelled and replaced by another from his parish. The Schoolmaster was not to take on the teaching of any paying scholars except by special licence from the Governors which was not to be granted if it was likely to result in any neglect of the interests of the free scholars – an important restriction on his freedom of action. He should ensure that 'the faces and hands of the scholars be washed, their heads powled and their garments kept clean' and every day two of them should sweep the school. Daily throughout the week (Sundays and festivals excepted) the boys should 'humble themselves to God in prayer upon their knees' in the school house, at 6a.m. 'from the Annunciation of our Lady until the Feast of St Michael the Archangel' and at 7a.m. in the rest of the year, and again, before leaving, at 5p.m. in Winter and 6p.m. in Summer.

Before taking up his appointment the Schoolmaster should be sworn before the Governors 'duly and diligently' to observe the Orders, on pain of dismissal for failure to do so, and he was required to give three months' notice of resignation. A register should be kept of all scholars, and an inventory of all the contents of the schoolhouse, to be accounted for at the time of the annual Visitation to the school by the Brewers' Company (see below).

Then followed the orders for the Almshouses. The Schoolmaster was appointed 'custos' of the Almshouses and of the almswomen, responsible for ensuring the repair and maintenance of the former (for which he was allowed 10 shillings a year) and for seeing that the latter fulfilled their duties and did not misbehave. The 10 almswomen were poor widows, aged over 50, 'of good name and fame and of honest, good and godly conversation and behaviour', chosen by Alice and after her death by the Brewers' Company from parishioners of Islington who had lived there for at least seven years, on the advice of the churchwardens. They were to be and remain 'single and unmarried'. Each almswoman had her own dwelling with a small garden attached and was paid 16s. 8d. a quarter for her maintenance. Each received annually on 'the feast of St John the Baptist' an allowance of coal for 'firing' and every two years at 'the feast of the nativity of our Blessed Lord and Saviour Jesus Christ' three yards of broad cloth to be made up into a gown, the cost being borne from the rents of the estate. They were required to attend prayers in the schoolroom twice daily. They were not to absent themselves from the Almshouses for more than three nights in the year without special permission and not to be out of their houses after 8p.m. in Winter and 9p.m. in Summer. They were to keep their 'yard' clean and were forbidden to admit any 'stranger' (i.e. non-resident) or sick person into their houses. Finally 'if any of the almswomen be a drunkard, a brawler, a blasphemer, a fornicator or a wilful contemner' of the rules, she was to be removed by the governors, i.e. the Court of Assistants of the Brewers' Company.

These Rules were to be read by the Schoolmaster to the assembled almswomen twice a year on the days following 'the Feast of the Annunciation of Our Lady the Virgin Mary and St Michael the Archangel'. Alice required the governors to keep a register of the almswomen and an inventory and detailed accounts for which tasks a Clerk and Beadle were to be employed. Alice also desired that the Master and other representatives of the Brewers' Company should 'once every year betwixt Easter and Whitsuntide' visit the school and Almshouses and should receive 30 shillings for a dinner on the occasion of the annual Visitation.[5] In a lengthy final provision, she committed the care of her School and Almshouses to 'the most honest and substantial fellowship of the Brewers of London ... trusting in the fidelity and love that they have to God and Man', and leaving it to them to make any amendments needed to the Rules. The texts of the Preamble and of the final provision are given in full in Appendix B.

The Schedule to Alice's Will, which is dated 23 September 1613, is headed: 'The distribution of the aforesaid revenues by me the said Alice Owen appointed as follows.' The revenues referred to are not only those intended for the School which are mentioned in her Will but also those arising from the property purchased to finance the Almshouses. Then follows a list of the expenses on salaries for the Schoolmaster/Custos, the Clerk and the Beadle, of allowances in cash and kind to the almswomen and for the running costs of the School and Almshouses, all precisely as specified in the Rules, including the allowance for a dinner at the Visitation. The total expenditure amounts to £72 a year. The Schedule, like the Will itself, was confirmed by Alice's mark (not signature) and was signed by the same three witnesses designated as 'scriveners'.[6]

The School and the Schoolmaster's accommodation were contained in the same building. The schoolroom doubled as the Chapel where the twice-daily assembly of almswomen and students for prayers took place. This was also the place where the Rules were read out annually to the almswomen. It was probably here too that the Brewers' Company representatives carried out the formal procedures connected with their annual Visitation, though they presumably adjourned to a more congenial location for the dinner. Nothing is said about the Schoolmaster's participation in this, but it must be hoped that he was invited to join them.

The main schoolroom was a single large apartment, sufficient to accommodate thirty to fifty boys, with several stools and benches and a long table for the boys to write on. At the far end of the room (opposite the entrance) was the Master's desk, a simple seat with two shelves above it. Lighting was by candles, which must have made it a pretty gloomy schoolroom in winter, and there was never enough coal to provide adequate warmth in a severe winter. The Master's personal quarters were over the schoolroom, up a staircase at the far end. They consisted of two small rooms, sparsely furnished, but possibly just about tolerable for a bachelor existence, especially, as Dare suggests, given the close proximity of the *Welsh Harp Inn* (or *Old Red Lion*) which provided warmth and comfort (though he would have to take care to avoid the offence of 'haunting of ale houses and taverns').

The boys entered the School at the age of seven and most would remain until twelve or at the latest fourteen. A few of the luckier ones may have spent up to two years at a petty school (where they would have learned to read, or at least the alphabet, with the help of an 'absey-book', though almost certainly not to write) before arriving at Owen's, which would have given them a start in the rudiments of language. At Owen's they would learn grammar, which meant Latin, not English, and to read and write in Latin; arithmetic, which is perhaps rather a sophisticated description of the elementary addition, subtraction and multiplication which was actually taught; and religious instruction, involving reading the Bible (in the newly published Authorised Version), reciting the Psalms, and learning the Catechism and Lord's Prayer, probably the only works in English the boys studied. The school day was a long one, beginning and ending with prayers as prescribed in the Rules. There were short breaks for breakfast, dinner and tea and brief holidays at Christmas, Easter and Whitsun, and time allowed to go to church on 'holy days'. With such a wide age spread and since a great part of the education consisted of reading aloud, oral presentation and answering questions rather than written work, the decibel level in the schoolroom must have been high and the schoolmaster's task a very exacting one. No wonder discipline was strictly enforced; it had to be. The Master had a cane visibly displayed beside him and it was often in use. But those who stayed the course of six years or so emerged with an education sufficient to enable them to move easily at the age of 14 into employment locally or to get taken on as apprentices in one of the City companies.[7]

Allowing for the completion of the School building and the selection of the first scholars under the Rules, the School could hardly have got going before November 1613. Sadly this meant that Alice would not have been there to see her great enterprise launched. She died in her house in Basinghall Street at the age of sixty-six. Though the exact date of her death is not recorded, internal evidence shows that it took place on 24 or 25 September. The cause of her death is not known, but she must have realised by the time she was working on the Rules that she had not long to live. Following her express wishes her funeral took place at St Michael's Church, Bassishaw on 26 September and, after an unaccountable two months' delay, she was buried in a vault beneath the aisle of St Mary's Church, Islington, on 24 November, these being the two churches with which she had been closely associated throughout her life.[8]

In her Will Alice left substantial legacies of money, jewellery and clothing to her four daughters; and she ordered that the proceeds of the sale of her house in Bassishaw and the residue of her estate should be divided among her three Robinson daughters. She evidently reckoned that Ursula Owen was sufficiently well catered for under her father's Will and with Condover and other properties inherited by her husband. In an imaginative gesture she bequeathed to each of the eldest children of her daughters – Alice Brett, Alice Rich, Mary Washbourne and Alice Owen – 'a chest of linen and such other things as are in the same chests', each marked with the girl's name. She also left a sum of money to each of her grandchildren. To her son, Henry Robinson, now installed as the squire of Cransley, she left about £4,500. And there were smaller bequests to her Wilkes and Draper nephews and nieces and to her goddaughter, Anne Bedingfield. In total Alice's monetary legacies to members of her family amounted to between £9,000 and £10,000, quite apart from the bequests in kind and the proceeds from the sale of her properties. This was a substantial sum. Any attempt to translate this figure into current values is fraught with difficulties – a rough approximation could be somewhere between £2 and £3 million.[9]

So much for the family. There were also legacies and bequests of apparel to her servants, including Ann Powell, who as suggested above was probably the one present at the arrow incident. Richard Wright, the ironmonger who had been Margaret Robinson's guardian at the time of her abduction (see Chapter 6) was acquitted of a debt of one hundred pounds owing to Alice! The customary provision of mourning gowns to 60 poor women, 20 of them to be residents of Islington, was also included. The latter would presumably have attended the burial at St Mary's Church, after which they would be given a free lunch.

Then came the charitable bequests and legacies, which were numerous. The Almshouses and School were built before her Will was written, at a prevent him from marrying, in 1678 – four months after his mother's death – Susanna, daughter of Sir John Ernle, Chancellor of the Exchequer, who was herself a strong adherent of the Church of England. One may surmise that the influence of his distinguished father-in-law may have helped to secure the removal of the sequestration order imposed on Henry's father during the Commonwealth. At any rate the manors, estates and advowson of Cransley were restored to him on the occasion of his marriage and he was granted a knighthood. Henry and Susanna had three children: Susanna, Henry (who died as a child) and John, the heir. In 1683 Henry donated one of the six bells installed in the church. Unusually all six bells were cast in the same year. Henry's was No. 3 and bears the inscription 'EX DONO HENRICI ROBINSON DO MILITIS 1683'. So perhaps in deference to his wife's views but also because of his position as Patron, he appears to have maintained a close interest in St Andrew's Church. By the 1680s the moderate Roman Catholic squirarchy were living on amicable terms with their High Church Tory neighbours and were increasingly alienated by King James II's attempts to revive Catholic supremacy and the old religious divisions.

In 1688 tragedy struck. Towards the end of the year Sir Henry Robinson became 'distracted'. One Sunday, after attending Mass at Desborough, Henry got up in the middle of the night, dressed and began to 'threaten and abuse his Lady'. Her cries roused the servants who managed to get him out of the bedroom, but he grabbed a large pair of kitchen tongs with which he made to attack them. They all fled, to return with reinforcements from the village who tried to restrain him. Henry was a large and powerful man and clearly terrified even this body of men. He armed himself with a small sword belonging to his son, with which he threatened to kill a woman he met in the street if she did not fall on her knees and pray to the Virgin Mary. By then the men had rallied, led by Henry's Steward who, on approaching him, was struck and wounded by the sword. The rest of the men managed to restrain him and bound him fast to a bed in the Hall. The local doctor could do nothing for him and as his fits and rages got worse, with periodic intervals of calm, he was despatched, tightly bound, by coach to London where it was hoped some treatment could be found for him. Susanna, presumably with the children, accompanied Henry to London and the household at Cransley was, for a time, broken up.

Evidently no cure was effected during what must have been an exceedingly unhappy period for the family (Sir Henry is said to have killed a maidservant at their London house). Eventually in December 1701, Henry was legally declared to be a lunatic and custody of his estates was given to his wife. She returned to Cransley, but the business of running the estates was effectively in the hands of her son, John. He added a large protruding two-storey bay with two windows on each bevelled side to take the place of the two middle windows of the five on the south front; and he replaced the existing front door on the east front, placing above it the Robinson arms, impaling Ernle (a band charged with three eagles) for his mother's family.

By Act of Parliament in 1710, the estate was vested in Trustees to enable them to make a settlement on John's marriage to Anne, daughter of Francis Duncombe of Broughton, Buckinghamshire. John inherited the manors and the advowson on his father's death in 1727. John and Anne had three children: Frances, Susanna and John. Anne died in 1737, her husband in 1748: both were buried at Cransley.

John, the younger, was admitted to Lincoln College, Oxford, in February 1737 at the age of seventeen. He did not take a degree, and his status as a 'gentleman commoner' suggests that he was not there primarily for the purpose of study. It is recorded that he spent two hundred pounds in a year at Oxford, a considerable sum for those days. In November of the same year he was admitted to the Middle Temple: whether or not he made any attempt to study law is not known, but there is no record of his having been called to the Bar. Evidently he set out to enjoy himself in Oxford and London which makes it all the more remarkable that he was made a DCL at Oxford in 1749. Unfortunately the grounds for this award are a mystery as the University records for the particular period in question are missing.

While supposedly studying at the Middle Temple, John's extra-curricular activities resulted in the birth of a baby girl in 1744. No birth certificate has been found for the child and her mother's identity is not known. The contemporary evidence for John's paternity is circumstantial but wholly convincing. The name by which she was, and has continued to be, known is Frances Brown. She is referred to as John's 'natural' daughter in a family history written during the lifetime of her grandson, William Somerset Rose of Cransley. Frances was brought up in the family of the Reverend George Burton, Rector of Elveden in Suffolk, who had a daughter of the same age. The link between John Robinson and the Burtons is admittedly based on some speculative assumptions about a series of relationships. But the speculation appears to be justified by the otherwise inexplicable fact that John Robinson was the principal signatory and George Burton one of the Trusteees of the generous settlement funded by John on the marriage of Frances to the Reverend Zacharias Rose, Curate of the parish of St James's, Bury St Edmunds, and descendant of a long line of Suffolk clergy, in 1772.

This is some years ahead of the point reached in the story of Cransley. There John Robinson married Dorothea Chester in December 1744, no doubt much to the relief of his father who would have been glad to see his son settle down before his death four months later when the son took over as Squire of Cransley. Dorothea was the fourth daughter of Sir William Chester, Bart, of Chicheley, Buckinghamshire. Her fortune was considerable for she inherited a sixth share of the large estates of Charles Wood (a cousin), of Loudham Hall, near Wickham Market in Suffolk, as well as property in Bedfordshire and Buckinghamshire from her father who died in 1725. On reporting the marriage the *Gentleman's Magazine* gave her wealth as £30,000, a good match indeed for the debt-ridden Robinson estate. Their marriage settlement has not survived but a lengthy supplementary document concluded in 1763 made detailed provision for an allowance to Dorothea in the event that she and her husband should separate, a somewhat unusual provision which may have implied a certain lack of confidence in John, especially as Dorothea, after 19 years, had failed to produce an heir. Dorothea, who was no doubt anxious to make amends for her own inability to maintain the Robinson line, evidently became reconciled to her husband's pre-marital indiscretion and accepted his daughter, Frances. She demonstrated her intention by arranging for Frances's husband to be appointed Rector of Cranford St Andrew, a village a few miles east of Kettering, immediately after their marriage. She was able to do this through the influence of her niece, also Dorothea, whose husband, Sir George Robinson, Bart (no relation to the Robinsons of Cransley) had purchased the advowson of the living.

Zacharias stayed only three years at Cranford before moving to Desborough, a few miles from Cransley, as Vicar. While he was there Frances's eldest child, John Capel Rose, was born at Cransley Hall and baptised at St Andrew's Church in July 1777 by his father, who described himself as 'Curate of Cransley'. Less than a year later Zacharias was appointed Vicar of Cransley by his father-in-law, John Robinson, who held the advowson. There followed two daughters, and a further move for Zacharias, to Broughton, near Cransley, where he died in 1790. Dorothea Robinson had died four years earlier without issue and her husband retired to live in Bath, where his daughter, Frances, joined him on the death of her husband. John Robinson died there in December 1791, the last ot the line of Robinsons of Cransley which had lasted just under two hundred years. The bulk of the Cransley estate was left to Frances and John Capel Rose, the latter having the residuary interest in the whole on the death of the other beneficiaries of John Robinson's Will. John Capel Rose became effectively the Squire and owner of Cransley Hall following his marriage in 1800. This took place in Bury St Edmunds, where Frances made her home soon after her father's death. She died four years later at Stonham Aspel in Suffolk, the home of her elder daughter. So began the line of the Roses of Cransley which lasted from John Robinson's death in 1791 until the estate was sold by his great-great-grandchildren (the grandchildren of John Capel) in 1905.[6]

Apart from two further bays on the north side of the front door and a further extension on the same side to accommodate a billiard room, Cransley Hall remains today exactly as it was in John Capel Rose's time (see illustration).

Ursula Owen had been mistress of Condover Hall with its 300-acre park since her marriage in 1609.[7] The estates belonging to Condover Manor included six hamlets in Condover parish and two smaller manors of Norton and Boreton which had been acquired by Thomas Owen and his son Roger. The parish, of which the boundaries extended beyond the Owen estates, was sparsely populated with fewer than five hundred adults in the early part of the 17th century. Apart from a few tradesmen in Condover village itself, they were nearly all engaged in farming. With the Lordship of the Manor went the advowson of the 14th-century church of St Andrew and St Mary to which Dame Alice had donated one of the bells.[8]

Roger Owen's duties at Lincoln's Inn and as Member of Parliament for Shropshire involved frequent periods in London during the next few years and, as already recorded, the couple's elder daughter was born there in 1612, when Ursula was staying with her mother in Bassishaw. Though he did not practise as a barrister, Roger was much respected for his legal knowledge and his literary ability. He played a major role in Parliament where he was an active champion of the clergy and often found himself siding with the opposition. But his radical and anti-Royalist views, which he had no hesitation in expressing, ensured that he was not re-elected after the 1614 session as Member for Shropshire where the gentry were predominantly Royalist in their sympathies. Roger, who was evidently a somewhat volatile character, was said by a contemporary observer to have become so excited on one occasion that 'his brains flew up and down in his head as a bird flies in the air'. Thereafter he and Ursula lived mainly at Condover where their second daughter, Sarah, was born in 1615. From then on Roger's health deteriorated and he died in 1617 'in a distracted condition', according to one account,[10] and was buried in Condover church. Surprisingly for a man of his legal background he was intestate so his family faced the problems of sorting out his estate. Condover Manor was inherited by Ursula and the Manor of Boreton, situated a few miles north-east of Condover, passed to her two infant daughters for whom Ursula was appointed guardian.

There is in Condover church a double monument erected by order of Jane Norton, Roger's sister and wife of Bonham Norton. It consists of two pairs of kneeling figures facing each other. Above are Jane and her husband and below Roger Owen, in armour, and their father, Judge Thomas. The monument was completed in 1541, the year after Jane's death.

Two years after Roger's death Ursula married Walter Barker of Shrewsbury. Like Roger Owen, Walter was a radical who took the side of the Parliament in the Civil War.[11] The Barkers moved into Haughmond Abbey, on the manorial estate of Boreton. The Abbey had been left in a ruined condition after the dissolution of the monasteries but Ursula and Walter converted the Chapter House into a residence for themselves and their children. Though Ursula remained Lord of the Manor of Condover until her death in 1629, Roger's younger brother, William, took up residence in Condover Hall.

It was at Haughmond that Ursula's five children by Walter Barker were born, all within the next ten years. With her two Owen daughters still only in their teens at the end of this period, this was a heavy burden even by the exacting standards of the time. At any rate it proved too heavy for Ursula, who died in 1629 at the age of forty-one. Some of her Barker children may not have survived infancy; her only descendants from her second marriage came from her daughter Cicely, who married Sir Henry Mildmay of Essex. Both Ursula's Owen daughters died in 1639 when Boreton Manor reverted to Condover, only to be sold out of the family a few years later.

William Owen, who did not become Lord of the Manor of Condover until Ursula's death, was nevertheless already a person of importance in the

County. He was appointed High Sheriff of Shropshire in 1623 and knighted in the same year. Unlike his brother Roger he was no radical and appears to have had no great intellectual pretensions. He was also a staunch Royalist, a firm adherent of Charles I in the Civil War and was taken prisoner when the Parliamentary forces entered Shrewsbury in 1644. He appears to have secured his release and managed to avoid losing his estates by payment of a very modest sum, and lived to see the restoration of the monarchy.[12] On his death in 1662 the Manor passed to his grandson, Thomas, and thereafter through two more generations of Owens. On the death of the last, with no male heir, it passed to his sister and was held by her descendants until 1896 when it was sold out of the family. In 1946 Condover Hall was purchased by the Royal National Institute for the Blind and since then has been a school for blind children. The photograph illustrated was taken in 1998.

This chapter has given a somewhat selective account of the fortunes of Dame Alice's children and some of their descendants. Much more could of course be said about the latter whose number must by now amount to several thousands. What is noteworthy, however, is that Alice left no-one to carry on the Elkin line; that her direct Owen descendants, through her daughter Ursula, had died out by the middle of the 17th century, and there were no more Owens of Condover after 1728; and that the last of the Robinson line died before the end of the 18th century. This is not to say they have not all had worthy, and sometimes distinguished, descendants. But sadly not one of those bears the name of any of Alice's three husbands through whom she acquired the means of funding her charitable works.